BRIGHT NOTES

PYGMALION
BY
GEORGE
BERNARD SHAW

Intelligent Education

IP INFLUENCE PUBLISHERS

Nashville, Tennessee

BRIGHT NOTES: Pygmalion

www.BrightNotes.com

ISBN: 978-1-645421-58-0 (Paperback)
ISBN: 978-1-645421-59-7 (eBook)

Published in accordance with the U.S. Copyright Office Orphan Works and Mass Digitization report of the register of copyrights, June 2015.

Originally published by Monarch Press.
Grace Horowitz Schwartz, 1965
2020 Edition published by Influence Publishers.

Interior design by Lapiz Digital Services. Cover Design by Thinkpen Designs.

Printed in the United States of America.

Library of Congress Cataloging-in-Publication Data forthcoming.
Names: Intelligent Education
Title: BRIGHT NOTES: Pygmalion
Subject: STU004000 STUDY AIDS / Book Notes

CONTENTS

1) Introduction   1

2) Textual Analysis   19
    Preface; Act 1   19
    Acts 2 and 3   33
    Acts 4 and 5   59

3) Character Analyses   78

4) Essay Questions and Answers   90

5) Critical Commentary on George Bernard Shaw   98

7) Selected Bibliography and Guide to Further Reading   107

INTRODUCTION

SHAW'S LIFE

George Bernard Shaw was born in Dublin, Ireland, on July 26, 1856. He lived for ninety-four years and wrote more than fifty plays. He is usually considered to be the greatest writer of plays in the English language since Shakespeare. He also wrote many volumes of literary criticism, art criticism and music criticism as well as numerous essays on social and political problems; an example of such an essay is the one called "The Crime of Imprisonment."

Shaw's family was part of the Protestant minority in Ireland, not the Roman Catholic majority. Shaw was himself baptized into the Church of England; however, he gave up formal religion early in his life, although he always had a deep interest in questions concerning the meaning and purpose of human life.

The Irish Protestant minority has always tended to regard itself as aristocratic and superior. Shaw's parents certainly felt this way. They were proud of their distant relationship to an Irish nobleman. In reality, however, they led a shabby, disorganized family life. The father was a grain merchant, and his business was always in difficulties; he was good-natured but ineffectual. He found life easier when he kept himself in a state of alcoholic confusion. His wife became an embittered woman who despised her husband and neglected her three children. She was much interested in music; so occupied was she with training her voice and arranging musical scores that she could not spare much time for running her household. George Bernard Shaw and his two sisters were neglected as children. When he was a grown man he recalled vividly how he had spent many childhood days in the kitchen, being looked after by a miserably paid servant girl, and how his meals had almost always consisted of badly stewed beef and stale strong tea.

The one thing he received in his home was a deep knowledge of music and a great love for it. While still a boy he knew many opera scores almost by heart. He could sing a number of passages from great operas note for note. He wanted to be a great singer, but he did not have the voice. His voice was good enough and well trained enough to make him an excellent public speaker in later life, however. Also, he learned enough about music in his boyhood to give him a foundation for writing about it; he became a music critic when he was in his thirties—some feel the best one that ever lived. In an amusing essay, the first thing he wrote after he got the job, he explains how his childhood qualified him for the job, although his knowledge of music had nothing to do with his being hired!

In his neglected boyhood, Shaw received a little Latin instruction from an uncle who was a good teacher. But his main education came from his own independent wanderings in picture galleries and museums, and from attendance at concerts, operas and Shakespeare's plays whenever he got the chance. Shaw's knowledge of Shakespeare was solid and detailed.

Shaw was sent to several different schools, always for short periods of time, and he cordially hated all of them. When he was

fifteen, he left school forever. This boy, who was to become one of the great masters of the English language, became an office boy in a Dublin real estate office. Here, among other things, he had the ugly job of collecting rents in slum tenements—an experience he remembered and put to use in his plays.

At nineteen, he moved to London. There he lived with his mother, who had left his father and was making her living by teaching singing. During his early years in London, Bernard Shaw determined to become a writer. He went about it in a practical way: he learned to write by writing. Between 1879 and 1883 he wrote five pages every day, eventually completing five books in this way. Unfortunately, the books were novels, for which Shaw had little talent. Only one of them has ever gained any popularity. That is *Cashel Byron's Profession*, a wildly comic story about a prize fighter. The others were pretty terrible.

Another important event in Shaw's life took place in 1882. He became converted to socialism. The injustices of industrial society in the nineteenth century, such as the labor of small children in factories and mines, the payment of wages too low for anyone to live on, the absence of sanitation and decent housing, made a deep impression on Shaw, as they had on Charles Dickens and Elizabeth Barrett Browning. Also, there was a depression in the eighteen eighties, so that Shaw saw plenty of cold, hungry people in London. Shaw was convinced by a lecture given by the economist Henry George, who felt that the inequalities of the economic system could be corrected by land reform. In 1884, Shaw read and was impressed by Karl Marx. However, he fought bitterly with the Marxists afterward. He became convinced that none of them had read Marx. It is interesting that to this day many Marxists are hostile to Shaw. They are stronger enemies to him than conservatives are.

Shaw joined the Fabian Society in 1884. This organization was determined not to make noble declarations about economic reform but to do something about it. This could be accomplished by getting to work on speeches and pamphlets that would convince others and lead to new laws. Shaw worked for many years with this small band of serious intellectuals. The Fabian Society played an important role in the founding of the Labor Party, today one of the two major political parties in Great Britain.

During these years Shaw knew about economic hardship from personal experience. His sleeves were so threadbare that he had to trim them with scissors; his hat was so worn that he was afraid to touch it for fear that it would fall apart. But better days were coming. In 1888, he began his brilliant career as a music critic. In 1895, he became drama critic on the London *Saturday Review*. His witty, intelligent, powerfully expressed reviews were of such excellence that it is still a pleasure to read them, even though the actors he wrote of are long dead and many of the plays mentioned are no longer known to most of us.

Through his friend William Archer, a well-known critic, Shaw became interested in the plays of the Norwegian Henrik Ibsen. Ibsen was causing a revolution in the theater by using plays to discuss and advocate new social ideas. This meant that the theatre was becoming a place where the audience could find stimulation for their minds, whereas before Ibsen there was nothing more to attract intelligent people to the average play than there is in a historical movie epic of our own day. Soon Shaw was writing his own plays under Ibsen's influence. The first one was *Widower's Houses*. This was about a subject Shaw was acquainted with at first hand—slum landlords. Its merciless attack caused a great furor in the newspapers. It had a run of only two performances in the little experimental theater where it was produced in 1892. England was not yet accustomed to anything stronger than milk and water on the stage. Shaw the dramatist was not exactly famous, but people were certainly starting to hear about him.

Now Shaw began to embody his ideas in comedy. By 1897 he had written *Arms and the Man, The Devil's Disciple*, and *Candida*. He was a rich and famous playwright. In 1898 he gave up his job as drama critic so that he could devote all his time to writing plays. *Caesar and Cleopatra* was written in that year. Also in 1898 he married Charlotte Payne-Townshend, with whom he enjoyed a congenial companionship until her death forty-five years later. By 1915, Shaw was famous the world over. He won the Nobel Prize for literature in 1925, an honor enjoyed by only three other Englishmen—Rudyard Kipling, John Galsworthy, and Winston Churchill.

George Bernard Shaw died in England on November 2, 1950.

SHAW'S PLAYS

Shaw wrote over fifty plays, more than Shakespeare who wrote thirty-seven, and far more than any other important English playwright. He began his playwriting career in his thirties. His great play about Joan of Arc, *Saint Joan*, was written when he was sixty-seven. In his eighties and nineties he was still producing interesting plays. Like such artists as the sculptor and painter Michelangelo and the opera composer Giuseppe Verdi, he continued to be creative even when he was a very old man.

There were no great English playwrights in the nineteenth century before Shaw. The best writers wrote poetry or novels. There were numerous actors of great skill and there were highly elaborate productions, but all this was wasted on plays that were worthless or on productions of Shakespeare's plays so chopped up and altered that they were hardly recognizable. It is no wonder that Shaw was inspired by Henrik Ibsen, the somber Norwegian whose extraordinary dramatic skill was used to treat controversial subjects in such a way that audiences were simultaneously angered and stimulated.

Shaw set out to do the same thing as Ibsen in English, but he soon found out that his own ability was better suited to comedy than to problem plays. After his first efforts, Shaw wrote comedies almost exclusively.

Shaw's comedy has nothing at all to do with slapstick or nonsense. These are good kinds of comedy, but they are not Shaw's kind. Shaw's method of comedy is to take familiar ideas and situations, to present them with a fresh and startling viewpoint, and to give new insight into humanity by doing this. For instance, *Pygmalion* tells a familiar story of the Cinderella type. We should expect a "happy ending" with Higgins marrying the transformed Eliza. But Shaw, with startling intellectual clarity, does not have them marry. Eliza has come to care for Higgins, but she does not really *like* him; he knows too much about her. Higgins cares for Eliza in the sense that he will find it hard to do without her, but if he gives in to this feeling it will be against his will. Then too, in some ways Eliza is Higgins' superior. She has a soul more responsive and sympathetic than his. Cinderella is changed in more than externals.

It is just because Shaw writes a conventional, familiar type of play that his unconventional treatment of the story is so stimulating. This treatment is embodied in confrontations between important characters, giving them the opportunity to show up each other's absurdities. It is shown as Mrs. Pearce discusses Higgins' bad manners with him. Another example is Alfred Doolittle's discussion with Higgins and Pickering as he talks them out of five pounds. Most noteworthy is the brilliantly written verbal battle between Eliza and Higgins in Act V.

Shaw brings out human foolishness and inconsistency with a bubbling gaiety which is one of his most noticeable qualities. He never ceases to be amused at human behavior, still more at human thought. We may surely conclude that Shaw delights in the innumerable absurd human types, that he loves life and enjoys living it. His writing could not have such vivacity and gusto if this were not so.

Yet Shaw's purpose is in the end like Ibsen's, even if his cast of mind is so different. For him, a play is a place to come to grips with serious ideas, to present new and sometimes startling points of view to the audience. For him, the stage is a place where the dramatist may teach and even preach, and the theater is a school and even a universal church. In portraying a character like Alfred Doolittle, for instance, Shaw manages to entertain and indirectly lecture to his audience at the same time.

Shaw's comedies cover a wide range of subjects. This lively-minded, sharp-witted Irishman is interested in almost everything, from socialism to marriage to medicine to religion, right up to and including kindness to animals. (In one of his stage directions, for example, he describes a female character who is wearing a hat "with a dead bird in it." It is hard to imagine a shorter or more effective attack on the practice of killing animals to get their feathers or skins.)

Because of his long interest in socialism, Shaw often deals with money and property in his plays. Shaw is convinced that much evil human behavior is the result of evil economic conditions. *Major*

Barbara is the most important of Shaw's plays on this subject. The class system is another frequent target of Shaw's attack; *Pygmalion* and *Misalliance* are two plays concerned with this.

A Note on The Actors In Shaw's Plays

The plays of Bernard Shaw are *stage* plays; they are splendid to read but they are made to be seen. Shaw knows just what will "go" when a play is performed—what dialogue and action will help it to move swiftly and keep the attention of the audience. One of the reasons why Shaw is able to do this is that he wrote many of his plays for special actors. When he wrote a play, he had the actor in mind as he worked. This kept Shaw's thoughts closely attached to the staging of the play. *Caesar and Cleopatra*, for example, was written for Sir Johnston Forbes-Robertson, a famous nineteenth-century actor. Forbes-Robertson's own natural dignity and majestic personality no doubt helped Shaw to some extent in creating Caesar.

What was true of actors was also true of actresses—truer, since Shaw had a habit of falling in love with actresses and writing plays for them as a sign of his affection. (Actresses also had a habit of falling in love with him. This fact has significance, not only gossipy interest; we must remember that the eloquent redheaded reformer and playwright was attractive to some of the most admired women of his day, especially when certain critics claim he does not understand the subject of sex.) *The Man of Destiny* and *Captain Brassbound's Conversion* were written with Ellen Terry in mind. *Pygmalion* was Shaw's gift to Mrs. Patrick Campbell. Both were famous and beautiful actresses. The correspondence Shaw exchanged with these two women constitutes two of the most famous sets of love letters in the world. Their wit makes them far more than conventional love letters.

SHAW'S LITERARY STYLE

Literary style is the way a writer has of using his language. It includes such things as choice of words, and the length and shape of sentences. Bernard Shaw's style does not call attention to itself by such devices as elaborate vocabulary or highly rhythmical sentences. The only special quality of the writing is that it mirrors the special quality of Shaw's mind—that is, it is exceptionally clear, lively, and intellectually powerful. It is obviously the result of Shaw's concentration on what he has to say. Language that is fancy or tricky for its own sake is of no interest to him. Students who are reading Shaw's plays are very often studying writing in the same English class. They could not do better than to take his straight-forward, vigorous prose as a model.

READING SHAW'S PLAYS

Shaw's plays make enjoyable reading because the author supplies not only the dialogue but much connecting material. There are full descriptions of the characters, vivid descriptions of the scenes, and numerous comments by Shaw which are often very entertaining. Shaw was the first playwright to do this. He felt that the ideas in his plays should be spread as widely as possible. Therefore he wanted to cultivate a reading public as well as a theater-going public. With this in mind, he made his plays as attractive to read as he could.

THE PYGMALION MYTH

Shaw takes the title of his play from a well-known Greek myth. There are two versions of it. In one Pygmalion is a king who falls in love with a beautiful statue. He prays to Aphrodite, the goddess of love, for a wife as beautiful as the statue. Aphrodite brings the statue to life. Pygmalion marries her.

In the other version of the story, Pygmalion is a sculptor. He makes the beautiful statue himself. He falls in love with his own creation and prays that life may be granted to it. The gods give him his wish. The statue becomes a living girl named Galatea, and Pygmalion marries her. Shaw uses the latter version.

In the play, Professor Higgins is Pygmalion. Eliza Doolittle is the woman he creates and gives life to. As in the myth, Higgins creates a beautiful object out of crude raw materials, but the last great gift of a living soul is more than he has power to give by himself. We do not quite know how it comes to Eliza, although Higgins has something to do with it and so does the courteous behavior of Colonel Pickering. Eliza herself is concerned in its creation. Ultimately, as in the original myth, it is a kind of miracle. Whether Pygmalion is to marry Galatea after the play is ended is not clear, and it is the subject of disagreement among readers, critics, and audiences.

PYGMALION AS A CINDERELLA STORY

As is easily seen, *Pygmalion* has a strong resemblance to the old fairy tale of Cinderella as well as to the Greek myth mentioned above. Eliza Doolittle is a perfect embodiment of Cinderella. She begins as a lowly, dirty creature. Then her transformation takes place. She is clean. Fine clothes are bought for her. She exhibits the behavior of a duchess. (Most important of all, her speech is changed. To Shaw, this is the most important part of the fairytale transformation from flower-seller to duchess, though the original fairy tale has nothing to say about it.) At last, she becomes the sensation of a great ball, magnificent in fine clothes and jewels.

Thus, the main action of *Pygmalion* is pleasantly familiar to all of us. It is also a story with a wide appeal. As Cinderella defeats her step-sisters, young readers cheer the success of the humble and despised one. The underdog enjoys a classic triumph. Besides, the story contains the appealing element of the impossible becoming possible. The wildest reversal of fortune occurs. It is the very essence of romance. This is always a comfort to ordinary individuals; they do not believe such stories whole-heartedly, but nevertheless they like to hear about such dramatic triumphs of the poor and the lowly. For thus it is shown that marvelous good fortune can happen to anyone.

To make use of a familiar appealing story like this is characteristic of Shaw's dramatic method. He assures our sympathetic attention by telling us a story that we like to hear, but he then uses our acceptance to further his own ends by adding material that challenges our comfortable ideas.

In this story, Eliza is clearly Cinderella. Higgins and Pickering are a pair of fairy godfathers. But these fairy godfathers cause as much pain to Eliza as they bring happiness. And then, who is Prince Charming? Is it Freddy Eynsford-Hill? Must the handsome. charming prince be a stupid prince? Or is it Professor Higgins? Does he combine the roles of godfather and prince? Worst of all, if it is he, will he fail to sweep Cinderella off her feet, marry her, and live happily ever after? What are we to make of Alfred Doolittle? He is surely a wicked parent. (We observe that Eliza is also provided with a stepmother, like a genuine Cinderella, but she never appears on the scene. Doolittle takes over her part in the story.) Yet it is most disturbing to our conventional ideas to find him a jolly rogue, whom we cannot help liking.

Thus we begin with an enjoyable, conventional story. We find that in it is concealed a devastating attack on polite society; Eliza changes her class by changing her vowels and consonants. However, to become a human being, Shaw says, is far harder than to become a duchess. Eliza does not accomplish this until the end of the play. Shaw also, presents us with a searching analysis of human relations far less soothing than the simple conclusion: "They lived happily ever after." Finally, in the person of Alfred Doolittle, we are confronted with difficult questions about poverty and morals. In summary, we may say that Shaw incorporates the fairy tale of Cinderella into his play. As we respond to its timeless appeal, we find that Shaw uses it as a method of presenting challenging ideas as well.

THE PLAY IN PRODUCTION

Shaw wrote *Pygmalion* in 1912 as a starring play for Mrs. Patrick Campbell, a gifted English actress. However, the idea had been working in his mind for years before that. In 1897 Shaw mentioned in a letter to Ellen Terry, another famous actress who appeared in several of his plays, that he had an idea for a play about an East End girl (the East End was a slum district of London) in an apron and three ostrich feathers. We cannot tell what kind of a play Shaw was thinking of then, but the physical image of Eliza was already formed in his mind.

By 1912 Shaw had written many of his finest plays. He had a world-wide reputation. But his reputation was greater on the continent of Europe and in America than it was in Great Britain. British reviewers would often attack his plays as being full of nonsensical ideas and then admit that they were entertaining anyway. Shaw was finding it wiser to open his new plays in other cities, where they were assured of excellent receptions, and then to bring them to London.

Accordingly, *Pygmalion* had its world premiere in Vienna in October, 1913. There was another opening in Berlin in November. Then, in rapid succession, the play was produced in Stockholm, Prague, Warsaw, Budapest, and New York (this last being a German language production in a small local theater). At last the play had its first English language production in London, in 1914, with Mrs. Patrick Campbell playing the role of Eliza and Sir Herbert Beerbohm Tree as Higgins. Then it came to Broadway with Mrs. Campbell.

Since that time, *Pygmalion* has provided a great role for many leading actresses, such as Gertrude Lawrence. In 1938 a film version was made in which Leslie Howard played Higgins and Wendy Hiller was Eliza. It was the first film of a Shaw play; the excellence of the result was probably because Shaw supervised the production personally. The spectacular success of *My Fair Lady*, a musical comedy based on *Pygmalion*, requires no description. This too eventually became a motion picture.

ORIGINAL SCENES AND ADDED SCENES

Most modem editions of *Pygmalion* contain added scenes Shaw wrote for film production or elaborate stage production of the play. These scenes are marked off from the scenes of the original play by asterisks. It is, therefore, possible to read the original version of the play by skipping such scenes, or to read the enlarged version by including them. The added scenes include Eliza's first bath and also her triumph at the ambassador's reception.

A SHORT INTRODUCTION TO PHONETICS

Nature And Background Of Phonetics

Henry Higgins, the hero of *Pygmalion*, is a professor of phonetics. That is, he is an expert on human speech sounds, the way they are produced, and the means by which they are perceived. The scientific study of speech sounds began in the nineteenth century. One of the pioneers in this field was Henry Sweet, a scholar at Oxford University and one of Shaw's friends. Shaw's portrait of Higgins is in some ways based on Sweet, who was a man of notoriously uncertain temper and eccentric behavior.

The Importance Of A Phonetic Alphabet

As soon as English scholars tried to study human speech in a systematic way, they found that they were severely handicapped by the English alphabet. Although our alphabet has twenty-six letters, the individual sounds in English number a good deal more. Thus, one letter had to be used to represent more than one sound. This made it impossible to record the actual sounds of spoken English accurately. For instance, the letter "a" represents quite different sounds in "father," "bat," and "fate." The scholar could, of course, put various marks over the letter "a" to symbolize different sounds, but this never proved entirely satisfactory. What was needed was a new kind of alphabet—a phonetic alphabet. A phonetic alphabet is one so designed that each sound is represented by one distinct symbol. When such an alphabet exists, it is possible to record human speech with some precision. That is, the person who knows a phonetic alphabet can write down, not the words someone is saying, but the sounds he is making.

The International Phonetic Alphabet

Henry Sweet was one of the phoneticians who helped to invent the International Phonetic Alphabet, which is sometimes known by its initials, IPA. This alphabet is even today the most widely known and used phonetic alphabet. It is an invaluable tool in many kinds of language study. It uses many of the letters of the regular Roman alphabet. In addition, it provides new symbols where there are no letters to represent differing sounds. For instance, with this alphabet we can represent the different sounds of "a" in "father," "bat," and "fate."

The Practical Uses Of Phonetics: Dialect Studies

One use which may be made of phonetics is the study of different dialects. A dialect is a local form of a language which differs noticeably from the standard form of that language in pronunciation, in vocabulary, and in other ways. In the United States, we speak of Southern dialect, a Western dialect, a Midwestern dialect, and others. The more expert a student of language is, the more dialects he can distinguish. For instance, for most Northerners, there exists simply "Southern dialect." But to the phonetician, who is skilled in analyzing sounds, there are many Southern dialects. A South Carolina dialect is not at all the same thing as a Louisiana dialect or a Texas dialect.

Professor Henry Higgins seems to be chiefly interested in dialects. He is so expert at detecting sound differences that he can distinguish between the dialects spoken on different streets of the city of London. He does this by writing down samples of speech as various Londoners speak them. He then analyzes and compares the different samples. He also uses sound recordings. As Higgins explains to Colonel Pickering, the practical applications of this knowledge can be very profitable. Higgins can teach a speaker of dialect English to change the sounds that he makes and produce the sounds of cultivated standard English. People who come from poor backgrounds but have become rich will pay a great deal to learn this, for they reveal their lowly beginnings every time they open their mouths.

The Practical Uses Of Phonetics: Spelling Reform

Shaw mentions the relation between spelling and phonetics in the preface to *Pygmalion*. English spelling was originally phonetic in nature. That is, one letter or one combination of letters represented just one sound. A person who wanted to spell a word would simply figure out for himself what the sounds of that word were and write down the letters for those sounds. Thus, there was no such thing as a "correct" spelling for any word. If a word could be recognized by the reader, it was correctly spelled.

This process continued for many centuries. At the same time, some people found it easier to copy the spellings of others, rather than to go to the trouble of inventing their own spellings for every word. But the idea that we must use a certain spelling, and only that spelling, for every word is quite modern. It came about with the publication of the first great dictionaries of the English language, those of Doctor Samuel Johnson (1755) and Noah Webster (1828).

But even after the standardization of spelling, spoken speech continued to change. For this reason, the spellings we use may represent pronunciations we no longer use. As English spelling now stands, it often has little relation to pronunciation. In other words, it is unphonetic. For instance, the spelling of "through" has only a distant relationship to its pronunciation.

Such a situation has many disadvantages. Unphonetic spelling makes both reading and writing much harder to learn. There is a social stigma attached to poor spelling, though investigation has shown that no relation exists between intelligence and the ability to spell correctly. Also, foreigners trying to learn English have a great deal of trouble. They cannot figure out how to say a word by looking at the way it is spelled. There is no sensible guide to English pronunciation. It is almost necessary to learn the pronunciation of each word separately.

In other languages, such as French, German, and Spanish, it has been possible to maintain logical phonetic spelling. These countries have national academies whose statements about language are accepted as law by teachers and scholars. The governments of these countries have also reinforced the rulings of the academies by edicts from time to time. However, in England and America, there is no central authority on language, such as an academy, to make decisions about spelling. Dictionaries record the spellings that are used; they do not decide what spellings should be used. And the government, by tradition, does not interfere in such matters.

For the above reasons, English spelling remains impractical and unchanged. Perhaps even more important are public conservatism and inertia. We like our spelling the way we are used to it, and most of us do not have a clear understanding of how unsatisfactory it is.

Shaw's lifelong interest in speech and phonetics led him to believe in spelling reform (just as it led him to write *Pygmalion*). In his will he left a large sum of money for the purpose of promoting the adoption of a more efficient alphabet that would make phonetic spelling again possible in English.

The Practical Uses Of Phonetics: Shorthand

Bernard Shaw was a skillful practitioner of shorthand. He indicates this clearly in the preface to *Pygmalion.* He could write Pitman shorthand, a widely employed system of stenographic writing invented by Isaac Pitman in 1840, which is still in use today. Shaw points out that it uses geometric forms, which are slower to use than regular handwriting. For this reason, Shaw approves of Gregg shorthand, which is based on regular long-hand writing. However, his highest praise is reserved for the system invented by Henry Sweet himself, which never achieved much popularity.

All the above systems of shorthand are actually phonetic writing. They are based on the idea of writing down sounds rather than words. Sweet's system was, in fact, invented by him to serve as a means of phonetic transcription. He later extended its use to stenography.

To summarize, George Bernard Shaw was interested in elocution, dialects, spelling reform, and shorthand. All these interests were parts or aspects of his general interest in the subject of phonetics.

PYGMALION

PREFACE; ACT 1

PREFACE

Shaw begins this short preface by discussing the shortcomings of the English language. He states that the English people have no respect for it and do not speak it properly. Much of the blame is placed on English spelling. Because of it, no person, neither Englishman nor foreigner, can teach himself to pronounce English by studying the way it is spelled.

Shaw also includes casual reminiscences of various early phoneticians he has known, such as Alexander Melville Bell, who invented "Visible Speech," an early phonetic alphabet. (This was the father of Alexander Graham Bell, inventor of the telephone.) He also mentions Alexander J. Ellis, Tito Pagliardini, and Henry Sweet.

Sweet is discussed at some length. He is most important here because he is the real life source for Shaw's portrait of Henry

Higgins in the play. Shaw warns that Higgins is not a portrait of Sweet; nevertheless, there are touches of Sweet in the way Higgins behaves. Sweet was full of contempt for all who did not appreciate the importance of phonetics. He never made any effort to be pleasant to ordinary people. He had no care for his personal appearance. (All these characteristics are also present in Higgins.)

Sweet's system of shorthand, called Current Shorthand, is also mentioned. It was originally meant by Sweet to be a phonetic script for writing English accurately and logically. Sweet later extended its use to shorthand. Shaw points out that it was superior to Pitman shorthand and Gregg shorthand, but Sweet never knew how to market it commercially. Sweet used to send people he knew confusing postcards written in his own shorthand; Higgins does this too, according to the play.

Shaw acknowledges that the poet and phonetician Robert Bridges also has a small part in his portrait of Higgins.

He boasts that *Pygmalion* has been successful, though its subject is dry and its purpose is to teach.

He concludes by pointing out that the transformation shown in Eliza takes place all the time in real life. Anyone can get rid of his original dialect and re-learn his language-but it must be done with the help of a phonetic expert.

Comment

This preface is short and casual. Its tone is informal. It is loosely organized; one subject leads to another in the way that this happens in ordinary conversation, rather than according to strict logic. Yet it is important, for it takes up a number of points which have relevance to the play.

SHAW ON THE ENGLISH LANGUAGE

Shaw mentions what every serious student of the English language is aware of-that its spelling does not have much reasonable relationship to its pronunciation. Most of us know that this makes English difficult to spell, and, if we cannot spell well, we are liable to be looked upon as ignorant and unintelligent, often unjustly.

But Shaw is interested in the reverse of this problem. English spelling is no help in the study of English pronunciation. This makes English pronunciation very difficult to learn. This difficulty in turn helps to perpetuate the low dialects which immediately identify the speakers as humble ones of poor education. Such dialects are an important factor in the division of people into social classes. Shaw points out in a famous sentence from the preface that every time an Englishman opens his mouth, some other Englishman despises him.

In other words, one of the basic ideas in *Pygmalion* is that poor speech is a cause and symbol of a rigid class system. Thus it is a basis of snobbery. To do away with low dialects is to do away with a social evil. The seed of this idea can be found in the preface.

HENRY SWEET

Part of the preface is a tribute to the greatness of this famous, though peppery, phonetician, on whom Shaw based his portrait of Henry Higgins. The scientific study of phonetics, or the nature and formation of human speech sounds, was developed in the nineteenth century. Sweet was one of its great pioneers and one of the originators of the International Phonetic Alphabet. This alphabet was an invaluable tool in the study of phonetics, since it made it possible to write down speech sounds exactly as they were made by a speaker. It was only when such exact records of speech were available that careful analysis of the sounds of language could be made.

Sweet was personally eccentric. His intensive interest in his subject made him indifferent to ordinary social customs. He would not bother to be polite to people who did not know about phonetics. He would not waste time over tidy habits or personal appearance. Sloppy, impatient, and quick-tempered, Sweet was probably a trial to people who knew him. However, Shaw has preserved only the amusing aspects of his eccentricities in *Pygmalion*. He has thus secured for Sweet a pleasant kind of immortality.

SWEET'S SHORTHAND

Shaw devotes some space to a discussion of Current Shorthand, an invention of Sweet's. The fact that Sweet (as well as Shaw) was interested in shorthand points up the fact that shorthand and phonetics are closely related. Most successful kinds of shorthand are phonetic writing. That is, they represent sounds rather than letters or words. Shaw himself wrote Pitman shorthand fluently and even remarks in the preface that he is writing it down in Pitman. But Shaw was critical of Pitman because it required the drawing of geometric forms such as lines and circles. He regarded Gregg shorthand as somewhat better, since it was based on the familiar letters of the alphabet.

But to Shaw, Sweet's Current Shorthand was the best of all; the master of phonetic studies naturally produced the best phonetic shorthand writing system.

In an amusing reminiscence, Shaw recalls how he used to get shorthand postcards from Sweet out of which he could make no sense. Sweet would be fiercely annoyed when he had to give an explanation, though nobody but the most expert student of language could possibly have understood what he meant.

Higgins too writes postcards, which bewilder his mother. However, he also sends along other postcards which explain the phonetic postcards.

ROBERT BRIDGES

Shaw mentions that Higgins' love for the poetry of John Milton is a characteristic copied from Robert Bridges (1844-1930), who was Poet Laureate of England (1913-1930). Bridges helped to found the Society for Pure English, which had as one of its purposes the reform of English spelling.

THE PURPOSE OF PYGMALION

Pygmalion is, as Shaw puts it, a **didactic** play-that is, a play meant to teach. It has been an enormous success all over the world. Its popularity, said Shaw, bears out his theory that all great art must teach, and that art need not be unattractive just because it teaches. Here Shaw makes a passing reference to one of his most earnestly held beliefs. Shaw began his professional theatrical career as a dramatic critic in the 1890s. At that time, the great majority of popular plays were spectacular historical plays or unrealistic melodramas or ridiculous farces. Most of them were absurd and almost completely lacking in intellectual content. No person seeking something to satisfy his mind would go to the theater, except possibly to see a play by Shakespeare. And even these were so cut and changed that they bore little relation to the plays as Shakespeare had written them.

Shaw soon became convinced that the theatre would become entirely worthless unless it began to deal with ideas. Plays should not simply entertain: they should stimulate, even trouble, the audience. They should discuss the problems of society. Shaw carried out these theories himself when he began his playwriting career. His earliest play is about poverty and slum landlords. He never changed his conviction that a play could not be important unless it handled some issue of contemporary life; as he went on, however, he changed his treatment of such issues from serious to comic. Thus, he produced his characteristic work, the play that has witty dialogue, very funny situations, and, at the same time, a serious point of view.

REAL LIFE PARALLELS OF ELIZA'S STORY

Shaw states that such changes in speech as Higgins teaches Eliza are not unusual in real life. Many poor girls have gotten rid of their original dialects and learned beautiful speech in order to become actresses. Salesladies in fine London shops and maids in elegant homes speak two languages-standard English on their jobs, and the low London speech called "cockney" in private life.

Shaw throws in a final joke as he concludes the preface. As he warns that only an expert teacher can teach a person to replace a low dialect with cultured speech, he tells all the ambitious flower girls like Eliza to remember this and not try to imitate fine speech by themselves. The chances of a girl like Eliza Doo-little sitting down and studying *Pygmalion*, or indeed any of Shaw's plays, are probably slight.

The scene is the portico of St. Paul's Church in Covent Garden Market, London.

ACT I

Comment

A portico is a group of columns covered by a connecting structure at the top, or in other words a sort of huge porch, usually at the front of a building of classical type.

Shaw identifies the church as one built by Inigo Jones, a great English architect who worked during the first half of the seventeenth century. He studied in Italy and brought to England the revival of classical architecture which was one of the features of the Italian Renaissance. Many public buildings designed by him still exist.

It is 11:15 P.M., and a summer thunderstorm is in progress. Various people have run into the church portico to escape the rain. Among them is a lady with her daughter, in evening dress. Her son returns from an unsuccessful attempt to get a cab but is promptly sent off to try again. They are joined by a girl who sells flowers in the street and by an elderly gentleman also in evening clothes. Behind one of the columns of the portico another man, his back to everyone, is writing in a notebook.

Comment

Many of the major figures of the play are introduced to us here. They are brought into contact with one another for the first time. The device of the rainstorm is excellent, since it is a good reason for various people of entirely different backgrounds to be forced to stay together in the same place for a short time.

The family in evening dress will later be introduced to us as the Eynsford-Hills. Already we see that the mother is pleasanter than the daughter. Young Clara is bad-tempered toward her own mother and brother. She is haughty and rude to strangers. Freddy cannot get a cab; when he brings one at last, he finds that his mother and sister have already walked away to take a bus. All this could happen to anyone, and yet Freddy contrives to give an impression of weakness and inefficiency. Perhaps it is the way he allows himself to be bullied by his mother and sister that creates the effect.

Eliza Doolittle is here with her flower basket (we do not learn her name until Act II). She is an unlikely figure of a heroine at first sight. Shaw dwells lovingly on her dirty little straw hat, her old black coat, brown skirt, apron, and worn shoes. But she is lively and cheerful as she tries to sell Colonel Pickering a flower. She is, after all, very young, only eighteen or twenty, so that she has not been worn down yet by her hard life. At the moment of her entry into the scene, she is angry, because Freddy Eynsford-Hill has run into her and knocked over her flowers. But she knows how to get along successfully in her existence; she promptly manages to get paid back for the flowers Freddy has ruined. Mrs. Eynsford-Hill pays her, because she has heard Eliza address her son as Freddy. Therefore, she is anxious to learn whether her son has been associating with this unappetizing guttersnipe. Her bribe is wasted. Eliza has only called him

"Freddy" by coincidence; she might just as easily have called him "Charlie".

Colonel Pickering, the gentleman in evening dress, has a kindly disposition. He is fairly patient with Eliza as she bothers him to buy a flower, and eventually he buys a little peace by giving her a present of a few small coins.

Now a bystander warns the flower girl that the man with the notebook is writing down everything she says. She is terrified; she is sure this must be a policeman. She begs Colonel Pickering not to have her arrested. The man with the notebook comes forward. He brusquely denies any connection with the police. At Eliza's request, he shows her what he has written, but it makes no sense to her bewildered eyes. The man reads back to her exactly what she has said, using precisely her own pronunciation. He further astonishes the bystanders by telling several of them exactly what area they come from. He climaxes the performance by identifying Pickering's background. The rain has stopped. The ladies in evening dress go off to get a bus. Other bystanders also disperse.

Comment

Henry Higgins, the leading male character in the play, has been present from the beginning, but he has been a silent figure. His abrupt entrance as a participant in the action is all the more effective now by contrast. What he has written down is the flower girl's speech in a phonetic alphabet, an alphabet which has a symbol representing each different human sound. It contains certain symbols not present in the conventional alphabet. That is why Eliza cannot read her own words. (For a fuller explanation of phonetic alphabets, see the Introduction to Phonetics in the first chapter of this book.)

Higgins is also a student of dialects. His training has equipped him to hear sounds analytically and to hear small distinctions between similar sounds. He also knows in what part of England, even in what part of London, each type of sound is made. This enables him to tell Mrs. Eynsford-Hill, Clara Eynsford-Hill, Colonel Pickering, and several of the bystanders, exactly where they grew up and received their educations. To those untrained in phonetics, this ability seems uncanny.

Note that as soon as Higgins enters the scene, the action accelerates. His behavior is direct, his speech is almost always a shout, and his general vivacity moves the play along with gay rapidity whenever he appears. As a result of Higgins' presence here, several actions go on at once. A group of bystanders now takes a loud part in the proceedings. They comfort and advise Eliza. They are in turn angered and delighted by Higgins. They are consistent in that they always misinterpret what is going on. Their remarks usually miss the point completely. At the same time, Eliza sits with her basket next to one of the columns of the portico. There she produces at intervals a series of short speeches. They are delivered in an unhappy undertone, are addressed to herself, and concern the way the man with the notebook has mistreated her. The effect is highly comic because Eliza is so absorbed in this conversation with herself and so entirely uninterested in the uproar that is going on around her.

Since the storm is over, everyone leaves the portico except the man with the notebook, the flower girl, and the gentleman in evening dress. The girl continues to complain to herself. The two men introduce themselves to one another. The note-taker is Henry Higgins, a professor of phonetics; the other gentleman is Colonel Pickering, an authority on Indian dialects. The two men have long been anxious to meet. As Higgins explains to Pickering how he teaches millionaires of humble background to speak properly, he happens to use the flower girl as an illustration of what he is talking about. She is condemned to the gutter for life because of her vile dialect. He could change her English so completely that in three months she could pass as a duchess. The attention of the flower girl is caught by this dramatic statement.

Comment

From this small scene the play grows. It is the seed from which the three-way relationship involving Higgins, Pickering, and Eliza Doolittle develops. When Higgins talks about how he could pass off this dirty, ignorant flower girl as a duchess at an ambassador's garden party, he has not the slightest idea of putting such a plan into execution. He is only using this particularly dramatic example to demonstrate what can be accomplished by applying the science of phonetics in a practical way. But Eliza does not have a mind that is used to thinking about imaginary circumstances. Higgins has said that he could make her into a duchess-or, he adds ironically, even into a saleslady or a lady's maid, which requires better English. Eliza is not interested in becoming a duchess, but she would like to be a saleslady in a florist's shop, employment now impossible for her because of the way she speaks. As a result of Higgins' casual remark, Eliza will present herself at Higgins' house the next day to start lessons. She means to pay for them in a businesslike way. (Note how skillfully Shaw sees to it that Eliza learns Higgins' name and address; Higgins tells it to Pickering while she is present.)

Higgins' character is expertly outlined by Shaw in this brief scene with Eliza and Pickering. He is entirely unconcerned about Eliza's feelings. He shouts fiercely at her when her complaints start to annoy him. This is the first of many times that he will shout at her during the play. He refers to her as a squashed cabbage leaf. His eloquence and his finer feelings are all reserved for the English language. When he speaks of it he becomes a passionate idealist. To Higgins, English is not only the language of a noble literature, of Milton, Shakespeare and the King James Bible, but also the vehicle of man's humanity. Man has a soul, and his soul appears in his gift of speech. Thus, the English language is to Higgins a supreme spiritual treasure; he has no patience with those who do not treat it with the reverence it deserves.

To summarize, Higgins is characterized here as a man who has little understanding of human feelings, but whose comprehension in the field of his work is exceptional.

Higgins and Pickering go off together. As they leave, Higgins hears the church clock chime. He is reminded of God and of charity. Into Eliza's flower basket he throws a handful of coins. Freddy returns with a cab at last. He is naturally irritated when he finds his mother and sister have left. Eliza, elated by her unexpected wealth, takes the cab herself.

Comment

Certain terms used here require explanation:

Pharisaic: Shaw writes of a lack of charity, using the adjective "Pharisaic." This means "pertaining to the Pharisees." The Pharisees were an ancient Jewish sect who paid scrupulous attention to the outer forms and ceremonies of religious worship. Their name has come to symbolize those to whom the external part of religion is more important than the inner, spiritual part.

British Coins: The coins which Higgins gives Eliza are difficult to explain clearly in terms of their modern American equivalents. First of all, we must remember that in 1912, when this play was written, the British pound (usually written pound) was worth about five dollars in American money, rather than $2.80, as it is today. A pound contained twenty shillings, and a shilling contained twelve pennies, or pence (they still do, of course). Figuring the pound at five dollars, we find that a shilling was worth $.25 and a penny was worth $.02; we get the following values for the coins mentioned in the scene:

Sixpence = 6 Half-sovereign = 2 1/2 Florin = 2 Half-sovereign = 10 pennies = about $.12 shillings = about $.63 shillings = about $.50 shillings = about $2.50

In addition, we must keep in mind that all sums of money had several times the buying power in 1912 that they have today. Considering all these things, we can see that the money Higgins carelessly tosses to Eliza makes up quite a considerable sum and represents undreamed-of wealth to her.

Eliza: When Eliza is given what seems to her a fortune, her first extravagance is a taxi ride to the wretched room that is her home. She takes the cab that poor Freddy drives up in. Apparently taxis are a symbol of great luxury to Eliza. Throughout the play, this is referred to. After a lifetime of trudging wearily over London streets, she prefers to ride rather than walk whenever possible. The "pleasant stroll" enjoyed by many under-active middle-class people is no pleasure to Eliza.

Eliza does not wish to let Freddy know what a poor neighborhood she lives in. Therefore, while this elegantly dressed young man is present she will not give her proper address to the taxi driver. Instead, she orders him to drive to Buckingham Palace. This represents a pathetic naivete: after all, considering her looks and her employment, Freddy would hardly be surprised to learn that she lives in a slum (even if he had the slightest interest in her at this point, which he does not). And nobody could possibly believe Eliza has any legitimate reason for going to Buckingham Palace. This rather touching innocence is often displayed by Eliza before she is changed. Pickering responds to it instinctively by kindness and gentleness; Higgins is unaware of it.

In a second scene to be used in a film of the play, or in reading the play, we follow Eliza to her lodging. We observe how miserably poor everything is and we see Eliza undress and go to bed. She does this by removing her shawl and skirt and piling them on the bed for extra warmth.

Comment

Eliza in her miserable room with its empty birdcage and newspaper pictures on the wall is in fact Cinderella among the ashes, ragged and alone, before the coming of the fairy godmother.

PYGMALION

ACTS 2 AND 3

....

| ACT II

It is 11 A.M. the next morning, in Higgins' house on Wimpole Street. Here, in a living room equipped as a phonetics laboratory, Higgins and Pickering are enjoying a discussion of their favorite subject. Eliza arrives, as elegantly dressed as she can manage. She has come to hire Higgins as a teacher, at a shilling ($.25) an hour. She wants to get a job in a florist's shop. Pickering reminds Higgins of his boast that he can turn Eliza into a duchess and offers to bet against him, as well as pay all the expenses of the experiment.

Comment

Eliza. Eliza is a pathetic figure. She has devoted much effort to her appearance for this highly important visit. She still wears an apron, but this one is almost clean. Her coat has been brushed. On her head is a hat with three ostrich feathers of loud and clashing colors. She has washed her face and hands. It is no wonder that she is indignant when Higgins refers to her dirty and low.

Eliza is angered and puzzled by Higgins. He does not have even a hint of ordinary courtesy. He orders her about as if she were a dog that has been let into the living room. He barks out commands such as "Sit down," and "Hold your tongue." This is impossible for her to understand; she is a prospective customer, about to bring Higgins business. Surely he ought to be polite.

Also, she has never heard anyone speak like Higgins before. His talk has, to her ears, a wild quality. Later in this scene, she decides that he must be "balmy." She does not realize that Higgins loves to orate and enjoys his own extravagances of speech. She also assumes that he was drunk the night before when he tossed her a sizable amount of money; Higgins' kindness is as eccentric as his anger, and she does not know what to make of it.

Eliza's calculations concerning the proper price of lessons shows her mixture of ignorance and shrewdness. She knows someone who takes French lessons from "a real French gentleman" and pays eighteenpence (1 1/2 shillings) an hour. English lessons, she reasons, cannot possibly be worth as much as French lessons. Therefore, she offers Higgins a shilling (twenty-five cents) an hour.

When Higgins figures that Eliza's shilling is the equivalent of sixty pounds from a millionaire, she is thrown into a panic, figuring that, in some way she does not understand, she has promised to pay him sixty pounds an hour.

Higgins: Shaw takes great care to describe Higgins in detail in this act. He stresses his physical vigor and general attractiveness. He points out that though he is rude, thoughtless and bullying, he always remains likeable. The remarkable thing is that Shaw actually manages to carry out this description in the play. This is a most difficult thing to do, since a person who is crudely insensitive to others and always sure he is right tends to be disagreeable in real life. But Shaw makes it clear that there is no meanness in Higgins; his intentions are never bad. He is indeed, as Shaw says, like a grown-up baby who cannot be kept out of trouble.

Pickering: Pickering shows the kindness that will be characteristic of his attitude toward Eliza. Higgins roars at her to sit down. Mrs. Pearce adds a crisp command to the same purpose. Eliza is frightened by this, but she refuses to be bullied. However, as soon as Pickering offers her a seat in a courteous tone, she is soothed and sits down at once. He will often be more successful than Higgins in handling the girl, because Higgins bewilders her with his violent behavior, but she is reassured by Pickering's quiet, respectful manner.

Higgins is delighted with Pickering's idea. He determines to make a duchess of Eliza. Rapidly he orders Mrs. Pearce to take her clothes away and burn them, clean her up, and order new clothes for her. Everyone is uneasy at the reckless way Higgins gallops ahead with the plan, but he cannot be stopped or discouraged. He overrides all objections. Eventually, Eliza is taken away to be bathed by Mrs. Pearce.

Comment

Dramatic technique. In this scene, Shaw shows his command of playwriting technique. Close analysis shows that there is little action or conflict here. Eliza asks for lessons, and Higgins decides to give them to her. But there is no interesting drama without conflict, so Shaw manufactures some conflict. Eliza has come because she wants lessons, but she is so astounded by Higgins' dreadful manners and lack of concern for her as a person that she almost changes her mind and runs away. Mrs. Pearce and Pickering are both uneasy because of the ruthless way in which Higgins pursues his idea once he is attracted to it. They raise objections. Mrs. Pearce is obviously completely opposed. At last Higgins gets his way. All this creates the illusion of bustling action and the clash of personalities.

Higgins. He here demonstrates Shaw's description of him. He is like a small child with a new toy as the idea of transforming Eliza takes hold of him. Again and again he unconsciously reveals that he does not think of Eliza as a human being with feelings. He orders her to be scrubbed and then wrapped in brown paper until her new clothes come, as though she were a doll or some other inanimate object. When Mrs. Pearce protests that she has no place to put Eliza, he tells her to put the girl in the dustbin. He does not mean this, of course, but it does show his attitude. He also discusses her in a completely tactless way while she is in the room with him. Mrs. Pearce wants to know whether Eliza is to be given any money while she lives at Wimpole Street. Higgins replies that all Eliza's needs will be supplied, so that money will be unnecessary. If she has any, she will buy liquor with it. He is uninterested in Eliza's furious insistence that she does not drink.

When he meets resistance, Higgins resorts to coaxing and bribery. He promises Eliza chocolates, beautiful clothes and unlimited taxi rides. He invents fantasies in which men kill themselves for her and she marries the handsome heir of a noble family. (The young nobleman does not interest Eliza very much; the taxi rides are a real temptation.) He also coaxes Mrs.

Pearce to let him have his way. He suggests casually that she can adopt Eliza as a daughter; this should amuse her!

Nothing can withstand Higgins now that he has really determined to see whether he can make a lady of Eliza.

Eliza. She is a picture of comical confusion. Within a few minutes she has been told she will marry a nobleman; she has been offered taxi rides, chocolates, gold, and diamonds; she has been threatened with living among beetles and being beaten with a broomstick; and she has heard a fantastic description of her future, in which she will visit the King in Buckingham Palace, where she must make him believe she is a lady or else have her head cut off. She is convinced that Higgins is mad, except when some action or remark makes her suspect (quite wrongly) that an assault on her virtue is intended. But the chocolate and taxi rides sound tempting and she does want to be a saleslady in a florist's shop, so she stays in spite of everything. Also, Pickering addresses her as "Miss Doolittle," a new experience for her, which gives her a sense of her own dignity and worth.

Mrs. Pearce: This lady, Higgins' housekeeper, is a model of respectability and good sense. She has a strong character which cannot be swayed by Higgins. Doubtless through long experience, she is unmoved either by his tantrums or by his coaxing.

She will not cooperate in his enthusiastic plan until certain points are cleared up. First of all, what is Eliza's status in the household? Will she be a salaried employee, a member of the family, a guest, a servant? Can Eliza be made to understand exactly what she is doing? (Pickering too is concerned about this.) What of the future? What arrangements are to be made for Eliza after the lessons are over? This is the first mention of this question, which is so important to the ideas in the play. Higgins' mother will take up this **theme** more strongly later. Significantly, it is the female characters who are concerned about it. The men ignore it cheerfully in favor of the immediate present.

Mrs. Pearce is patiently insistent. She will not permit Higgins to evade her questions. Toward Eliza she is firm but decent and reasonable. She may have prejudices against taking a dirty flower seller from a street corner into her household; however, she realizes that the girl's failings are not her fault. Also she takes the trouble to talk to Eliza in order to make things clear to her.

A short scene follows, not for the stage version of the play, but for a screen version or for reading. Eliza gets her first sight of a bathtub as she is forcibly cleaned up by Mrs. Pearce.

Comment

We learn here that Eliza has never been washed from head to toe all at once. She has never had all her clothes off at once. This is not because she is a person who likes to be dirty. Rather, it is because she has had no bathtub, no hot water, and very little heat. She hates to be cold. The idea of sleeping in clean nightclothes in a warm, clean bed is beyond her understanding. The experience of the hot bath is terrifying. Eliza's screams echo in our ears as the scene ends.

Back in the laboratory, Pickering asks for Higgins' assurances that Eliza will not be taken advantage of. Higgins assures him that he has no personal interest in Eliza, or any female pupil in fact. Mrs. Pearce enters for a conference. She points out that Higgins swears habitually and has sloppy personal habits. He must reform in order to be a good example to Eliza. Higgins begins by denying Mrs. Pearce's statements but ends by agreeing to do as she asks.

Comment

Higgins and Women. Pickering delicately suggests the possibility that Higgins may find himself attracted to Eliza. Higgins says that it would be impossible for him to teach if he could not maintain strictly a businesslike relationship with his pupils. Anyway, he has taught American millionairesses, the best looking women on earth, and he is unlikely to be attracted to someone like Eliza if he was not attracted to any of them. Also, Higgins confides that he does not care for relationships with women. A woman with whom one becomes friendly immediately becomes a jealous nuisance. And the man becomes a tyrant. They pull in two different directions and then they end up taking a third direction as a compromise, one that neither of them wants. Thus Higgins is a bachelor; he intends to keep on being a bachelor.

Higgins' Eccentric Habits. Mrs. Pearce feels a heart-to-heart talk with Higgins is necessary if an impressionable young girl is to live in the house.

First of all, his language is terrible. He swears constantly. It is interesting to note that Mrs. Pearce is not worried by his use of the word "damn." What she objects to is the adjective "bloody." To Americans this is not at all a shocking word, but in England it was (and is) considered offensively vulgar. Mrs. Pearce will not even permit the word to pass her lips. She refers to it indirectly, indicating that it begins with the letter "b." Of course, it is well known to Eliza; she has heard plenty of rough language in her lifetime. But she is now to learn new and better behavior; this will be almost impossible if Higgins uses bad language in front of her.

Next, Mrs. Pearce takes up Higgins' table manners. He wipes his fingers on his dressing gown (in America usually known as a bathrobe) and is so careless in the way he handles food that last week a fishbone somehow got into the jam jar.

These eccentricities are probably taken by Shaw from the phonetics expert Henry Sweet, who was in real life as quick tempered and untidy as Higgins is in the play.

Higgins is pained and surprised at Mrs. Pearce's accusations. He first responds by becoming haughty and ends by losing his temper and yelling. It is amusing to see him try to cope with Mrs. Pearce; she will not allow him to deny his conduct or to change the subject. Our enjoyment is intensified by that of Colonel Pickering, who has a very good time watching the scene.

After Mrs. Pearce's departure, Higgins confides to Pickering that Mrs. Pearce misunderstands him. She considers him a bullying, loud sort of man, whereas actually he is exceptionally meek. This is not only funny, but a shrewd touch in the portrait of Higgins. In real life, we observe that the most domineering people are often convinced that everyone takes advantage of their gentle natures.

Now Alfred Doolittle, Eliza's father, enters. He exhibits righteous indignation, suggesting that Higgins has taken Eliza for immoral purposes. However, he is prepared to overlook this for five pounds (twenty-five dollars). But Higgins is more than Doolittle can handle. He shocks Doolittle by ordering him to take Eliza away at once. He accuses Doolittle of blackmail, threatening loudly to call the police. Eventually, however, Higgins becomes delighted by Doolittle's cheerful admission that he has no moral standards. He pays him the five pounds, though he and Pickering feel it is wrong to do so.

Comment

Alfred Doolittle. One of the methods Bernard Shaw uses to keep his plays lively throughout their length is to introduce new characters occasionally as a play progresses. This prevents us from getting bored with the characters shown at the beginning (for no matter how amusing they may be, they could become monotonous if we had nobody else to watch). It also offers us new and different individuals to entertain us and make us think. The introduction of Alfred Doolittle in Act II of *Pygmalion* is a good example of this technique.

Eliza's father is a dustman (a garbage collector). He also works as a navvy (laborer) occasionally. Doolittle is a thorough rascal. He cares nothing for his family responsibilities. It may be that Eliza is in some danger, for all he knows. But he looks on the situation only as an opportunity to make five pounds. He is addicted to drink and women (the lady he is now sharing his home with is referred to by Eliza as her sixth stepmother).

His redeeming feature is his complete honesty. He makes no pretense of having a conscience. He claims he cannot afford one. He states clearly his intention of using the money he hopes to get from Higgins for a wild week end spree. He has natural eloquence, a genial manner and a strong original intelligence. In fact, he is able to analyze himself and his ideas far better than a man like him probably could in real life. Shaw himself pointed this out. This is, Shaw states, a necessary dramatic device.

Many of Doolittle's ideas are unusual, to say the least. He classifies himself as a member of the Undeserving Poor. He likes being one of the Undeserving Poor; he is not going to change. But it does present problems. When there is something to be given away, the Deserving Poor are the ones who get it. Yet his expenses are higher than those of the Deserving Poor; he spends more on drink, for one thing. This is why Higgins' five pounds will be so useful.

Doolittle is not married to Eliza's sixth stepmother. Pickering reproaches him. Doolittle's surprising answer is that he wants to get married, but the woman is too smart to do so. Doolittle has no hold on her; therefore, he is forced to be pleasant to her; give presents, and buy her many clothes.

Higgins is quite won over by the amusing rogue; he offers him ten pounds instead of five. Doolittle is too good a student of human nature to accept it. Ten pounds is a tidy little sum of money. He and "the missus" might be tempted to save it instead of having a good time. Five pounds will suit his purposes better.

Doolittle and Falstaff: In a magazine interview published in 1920, Shaw pointed out an interesting parallel between Doolittle and Shakespeare's Falstaff. Falstaff is a fat, rascally knight who is a leading character in Shakespeare's plays, Henry IV, Parts I and II. He is usually considered to be the greatest comic character in English literature. In one of his most famous scenes, Falstaff analyzes honor: "What is it? A word." Falstaff weighs the importance of honor and comes to the prudent conclusion that, since soldiers who have gained honor are usually dead as well, he will have no part of it. Shaw remarked that when Doolittle analyzes his position as one of the Undeserving Poor and rejects morals because he cannot afford them, he sounds a good deal like Falstaff.

A Note: "Native Woodnotes Wild." Higgins uses this expression when he is describing Doolittle's way of speaking. It is a quotation from L'Allegro, a beautiful poem by the seventeenth-century English poet John Milton. Higgins' admiration for Milton is referred to several times; therefore, this quotation is suitable to the character. In Milton's poem, the expression quoted above refers to Shakespeare's poetry, which Milton regarded as the beautiful but untutored product of a natural genius.

As Higgins is leaving, Eliza enters, clean and dressed in a Japanese kimono, the only woman's garment Mrs. Pearce could find to put on her. Her father does not recognize her. Feeling incompletely dressed, she adds her hat to her costume. She is full of praise for the comforts of the bathroom, but the looking glass which reflected her undressed image embarrassed her terribly. Eliza makes plans to take a taxi to where she used to sell flowers, just to snub the girls she worked with. But she rushes off when her new clothes arrive; everything else is driven out of her head.

Comment

Eliza's growing self-awareness is brought out here. She is becoming very conscious of her appearance. She relishes the pleasures of cleanliness. Her truly feminine delight in new clothes is shown.

Doolittle's pleased surprise at how pretty Eliza is when clean is a funny touch. He has apparently never seen her that way, since he does not know her when she comes in.

Higgins urges Doolittle to come to visit his daughter and give her good fatherly advice. Higgins has a brother, a clergyman, who will be glad to help him do so. Doolittle agrees to this amiably but puts it off into the future, for right now he has a job that will call him out of town. Doolittle fades hurriedly out of the picture. This is Higgins' clever method of getting rid of Doolittle. When he is urged to come to Wimpole Street as a moral duty, he is sure to disappear, especially if he thinks he will have to associate with a clergyman.

There is a short scene, again meant for reading or for a motion picture, which shows Eliza's first speech lesson. Higgins strides up and down restlessly as he teaches her. She does very well, and he is pleased with her, though you would not know it from the way he shouts at her.

Comment

Eliza, clean, decently dressed, struggling painfully over her vowels and consonants, does not know it, but she is Cinderella getting ready for the ball. The professor of phonetics who bellows at her so fiercely is also a kind of fairy godfather. In a way, so is Colonel Pickering, as he observes and reassures.

ACT III

Comment

The first scene of this act (originally, in Shaw's play, it was the entire act) is Bernard Shaw's contribution to the basic Cinderella story. This scene occurs before the ball and Cinderella's triumph. It is her first trial in the glittering great world, and she does not quite make a success of it.

When the play is performed, this is the funniest and most successful scene. The role of Eliza is a splendid one throughout, but this scene gives the actress who plays her the greatest opportunity for evoking uproarious laughter from the audience, together with a delicate touch of pathos.

Eliza's enunciation is now a thing of beauty, though she comes down a bit hard on her "h's" in order to avoid dropping them altogether. Along with her precise formation of words, she also exhibits a lovely, cultured voice. The technical excellence of her speech is not the only change in her. She is beautiful. Her clothes are superb. She walks, stands, and sits with exceptional grace.

The only trouble is that her mind has not caught up with the rest of her yet. She knows how to speak but is ludicrously ignorant of what to say. The contrast between the elegance of her speech and behavior and the utter vulgarity of what she has to say is what makes the scene so comic.

Mrs. Higgins, Henry's mother, is preparing to entertain guests in her home. Henry Higgins bursts in to tell his mother that he has invited Eliza to visit her. The Eynsford-Hills arrive. He exhibits his usual dreadful social behavior. Pickering also arrives.

Comment

Mrs. Higgins' Room. Mrs. Higgins' drawing room (her reception room or living room) is described in detail. It is a room in excellent taste, decorated by Mrs. Higgins in the style admired when she was a young woman, rather than in the fashion popular in 1912, the time of the play. Several famous Victorian designers and artists are mentioned in the description:

William Morris. Morris was an English poet and artist who lived from 1834 to 1896. He was strongly attracted to medieval legends; he retold a number of them in long narrative poems. From this he moved to an interest in medieval handicrafts. He founded a company which manufactured wallpaper, textiles, glass, and furniture of beautiful design by long abandoned methods of careful hand workmanship. These items were extremely expensive, naturally. Mrs. Higgins has Morris wallpaper and fabrics in her room.

Morris also founded the Kelmscott Press, which published magnificent editions of early English writers, as well as Morris' own poems. He was a Socialist too, like Shaw. Shaw knew him personally when he was a young man; indeed, at one time he apparently had some intention of marrying Morris' daughter.

Edward Burne-Jones. He was a friend of William Morris. He also enjoyed a productive friendship with Dante Gabriel Rossetti, another English poet and artist. Burne-Jones and Rossetti were so delighted with the painting and decorative arts of the middle ages that they founded a school of art known as the Pre-Raphaelite Brotherhood. They tried to return in their painting to the kind of work done before the Italian Renaissance artist Raphael. They were attracted to romantic subjects set in distant times and places.

Mrs. Higgins was influenced by the Pre-Raphaelite ideas when she was young. She likes the dreamy, exquisitely colored paintings of Burne-Jones. In her room is a painting of herself as a young woman in a medieval costume such as Rossetti admired.

Cecil Lawson. He was a landscape painter who lived from 1851 to 1882. He created a number of large oil paintings, romantic and poetic in manner. Mrs. Higgins has one of these in her drawing room. Note also that Mrs. Higgins owns a Chippendale chair, made by the great English furniture maker Thomas Chippendale in the latter half of the eighteenth century. Chippendale chairs are usually made of mahogany in a design which is strong yet graceful, and distinguished by finely carved detail. The Elizabethan chair in the style of Inigo Jones (see Comment on beginning of Act I) would be heavy and massive, with large carvings for ornament.

Mrs. Higgins. Mrs. Higgins serves to enliven the play as Alfred Doolittle did in Act II. She is a new and different personality. She embodies the aristocratic virtues of elegance, graciousness, and sensitivity. In fact, she is totally unlike her son. Besides this, Mrs. Higgins stands in a totally different relationship to Higgins from anyone else in the play. Whereas he is a cranky, explosive genius to the others, who cope with him as best they can, he is a troublesome child to his mother. She regards him with an affectionate mixture of patience and exasperation.

An excellent comic touch is the way Shaw turns upside down this meeting between mother and grown-up son. Whereas we would expect to see the mother passionately happy to see her child, and even perhaps reproachful that he has not come more often, Mrs. Higgins is horrified to see Henry show up on the day that she expects visitors. She reminds him that he promised not to come and urges him to go back home immediately. We soon see why.

Higgins' Social Behavior. Higgins paces up and down, fidgets, and bangs into the furniture. He is a disturbing element in his mother's gracious home. He abruptly breaks it to her that he has invited a sidewalk flower seller to her "at-home" (this being a certain number of hours during the week when all the hostess' friends and acquaintances are invited to visit without the need of a specific invitation). As he is trying to explain to her Eliza's exact stage of development on her progress toward being a lady, the Eynsford-Hills arrive. The explanation is left incomplete.

Of course, the Eynsford-Hills are the mother, son, and daughter who were trying to get a cab in the first scene of the play. Higgins is irritated at their arrival. He tries to get away, but his mother is too quick for him. She introduces him to Mrs. Eynsford-Hills and Clara. His irritation turns to despair when Freddy enters the room, for anyone can see that Freddy, though amiable, is not too bright. Higgins mumbles to himself: "God of Heaven! another of them!"

Higgins is annoyed simply because he hates aimless chatter with strangers, not because he recognizes his mother's guests. He only does that after Eliza's arrival. He treats them with spectacular rudeness, making no secret of their hopeless stupidity and his boredom. He is still appealing even now, for he does not realize what he is doing. His reactions are not unkind. They display the innocence of a child on a visit who says: "I don't like that lady! I want to go home!"

The Eynsford-Hills. The portraits we have of this family are enriched in this scene. Mrs. Eynsford-Hill is a lady by social class, but she does not have the money necessary to uphold that position. According to accepted custom, she cannot earn a living; nor can her children; for ladies and gentlemen do not work for money. Therefore the family is constantly struggling to make ends meet. Mrs. Eynsford-Hill is perpetually worried; but she is a pleasant person. She tries to be friendly to Higgins, though he startles and bewilders her.

Her daughter Chara, who seemed ill-tempered in the first scene, becomes rather touching here. She feels perpetually out of place in society, because she is too poor to go out a great deal. But Clara puts on a brave show. She acts as though she were full of gaiety and self-confidence, when in fact she is quite unsure of herself.

Clara makes a great effort to get on friendly terms with Higgins. After all, he is a bachelor, and there is no harm in trying. We know that she is making a hopeless attempt, and we are both amused and sorry for her. Higgins cannot even bring himself to be normally civil to her. It is comic to think of his reaction if he were ever to grasp a hint of any suggestion that he consider marrying her. Freddy says almost nothing during the early part of the scene. He comes to life later when he is bowled over by Eliza.

The Relationship between Higgins and his Mother. Higgins' mother thinks at first that her son has comes to her house to tell her he has met a girl he cares for. She remarks that he does not seem attracted to any woman under forty-five years of age, as a usual thing. He replies that he only likes women who are like his mother. Besides, young women are idiots.

We might be justified from this in diagnosing an Oedipus complex. That is, one reason Higgins has not married is because he is so firmly attached to his mother that other women do not attract him strongly. Yet we should also remember that Mrs. Higgins does not act like the fiercely possessive, emotional mother who is usually the other party in an Oedipal relation. Besides, there are other reasons for Higgins' bachelorhood-his devotion to his work, for instance, and his self-centered nature.

Eliza enters. She is a pleasure to look at, and her speech is beautiful. Mrs. Eynsford-Hill and Clara are impressed by her elegance. Freddy falls head over heels in love with her on the spot. But her efforts at social conversation are ghastly. She tells a complex story about an aunt of hers who presumably died of influenza; Eliza is convinced the old lady was murdered. Just as she is really starting to enjoy herself, Higgins signals her to leave. She uses the vulgar word "bloody" just before her exit; this is the final **catastrophe**. But fortunately, the Eynsford-Hills think her talk is the latest popular fad.

Comment

Eliza begins her social debut well. She greets her hostess and her fellow guests in the proper manner. Her movements have obviously been taught to her with much care. She is, in fact, a reasonable facsimile of a lady, except that her pronunciation is a little too perfect.

We may say, in summary, that while Eliza is feeling stiff and frightened, she gives a creditable performance. But when she begins to feel at home, trouble starts.

She makes a remark about weather conditions, which she has carefully rehearsed beforehand. Freddy is amused and her grammar collapses. Mrs. Eynsford-Hill makes a kindly attempt to save the day by turning the subject to influenza; it is a natural outgrowth of the talk about bad weather.

Unfortunately, this reminds Eliza of her aunt. She becomes interested in what she is saying. No longer afraid, she tells her story, with dark hints about murder for the old aunt's straw hat. Her faux pas come thick and fast: she reminisces about how her father once saved her aunt from diphtheria by ladling gin down her throat. This leads her to a discussion of her father's drinking.

She discourses on how married life is improved by keeping the husband drunk and happy.

Her hearers are alarmed at her father's rough and ready treatment for her aunt's diphtheria. Was it not dangerous to dose her so vigorously with gin? Eliza reassures them cheerfully: "Gin was mother's milk to her."

This story, so uproariously funny under the circumstances, is yet pathetic in its unconscious revelations of the squalor of Eliza's life. All of it is told in Eliza's newly learned cultured speech; her grammar has not been much improved, but her pronunciation is perfection. The combination of all these elements is a comic masterpiece.

The **climax** of the disaster is Eliza's reply to Freddy's question about a walk across the park. To her, such a question is virtually an insult. Only poor people walk. Ladies ride in taxis. No doubt this accounts for her vigorous reply: "Not bloody likely!"

The use of this expression on the stage caused a sensation when *Pygmalion* was originally produced in London. Such vulgarity was unprecedented (at least in recent times; Shakespeare is quite outspoken); it probably had its part in initiating modern **realism** in the language of the theater.

It is difficult for non-British people to catch the flavor of the word "bloody." It is vulgar, offensive, but not indecent. The American slang word "lousy," though less objectionable, is perhaps a reasonably acceptable example of the same type of language.

On the heels of Eliza's sensational exit, the Eynsford-Hills depart. Mrs. Eynsfold-Hill is in a state of shock over Eliza's language. Clara is delighted to think that she has just learned about the latest fad. Freddy is infatuated with the beautiful Miss Doolittle.

Comment

Mrs. Eynsford-Hill seeks Colonel Pickering's support as she voices her distress over modern behavior. They form an alliance against the kind of language that has recently become acceptable. They as an older generation take sides against the younger generation, represented by Clara. Clara defends the new freedom of expression. It seems smart and gay to her. The poor girl does not realize that she is showing how out of touch with things she is. She does not go to enough parties and dances to know what is acceptable and what is not.

Higgins grasps the situation and mischievously eggs Clara on. He urges her to use the word "bloody" at the other houses she will visit during the afternoon. Clara departs, happily unaware that she is going to expose herself to embarrassment.

Colonel Pickering, on the other hand, tries to reassure Mrs. Eynsford-Hill, who is in a flutter because she thinks she will have to start using this "modern" slang. He points out that she does not have to say the objectionable word if she does not want to. The contrast between the behavior of Higgins and Pickering in this small scene is an excellent indication of the difference in their characters-Pickering kind and thoughtful, Higgins mischievous and irresponsible, although he means no real harm.

The sympathy of the audience is permanently secured for the Eynsford-Hills (even Clara!) by the mother's sad little speech of apology to Mrs. Higgins as they leave. Also, our insight into the wretched existence of this family is important; they are a living example of what can happen to people who have learned upper-class behavior but do not have upper-class incomes. This can happen to Eliza too, unless Higgins and Pickering can be persuaded to plan intelligently for her future.

Mrs. Higgins observes (for she does not miss much) that Freddy has been impressed by Eliza. She invites him to visit her soon, indicating that Eliza will probably be visiting too. Thus, we realize that Freddy will probably be seeing Eliza again.

To the eager question of Higgins and Pickering, Mrs. Higgins replies that Eliza will not pass as a lady yet; her language betrays her. Mrs. Higgins then asks for exact information about Eliza's position in Higgins' household. She points out that Eliza represents a problem. What is to become of her after the experiment is over? Neither Pickering nor Higgins takes this very seriously. They depart, leaving Mrs. Higgins thoroughly exasperated with their shortsightedness.

Comment

Mrs. Higgins acutely points out that as long as Eliza keeps hearing her son's language, she will have difficulty in learning what words are socially acceptable. Higgins, as usual, is vastly insulted at any suggestion that he uses bad language.

Note: Pickering speaks of removing the "sanguinary element" from Eliza's conversation. Sanguinary means "bloody." Pickering is thus referring delicately to Eliza's error. He is also making a small joke or witty remark.

Mrs. Higgins' mind runs along the same track as that of Mrs. Pearce in the second act. She tries to get precise information about the terms on which Eliza lives in her son's home. Is she a servant? If not, what is she? She is not content with the casual, unplanned nature of Eliza's status. She is particularly concerned because the men have given no thought to Eliza's ultimate destiny. (Note that Mrs. Pearce is having similar thoughts. Higgins reports that she says to him constantly, "You don't think, sir", whenever they discuss Eliza.)

Higgins and Pickering are indignant at Mrs. Higgins' reproaches. How can she suggest that they do not think about Eliza? They think of nothing else! They think of her vowels, her consonants, her manners, her clothes. They enjoy her unsuspected talents: she has a remarkably quick ear and can imitate difficult sounds. Also, she is musical, playing by ear anything she hears, whether it is Beethoven, Brahms, Lehar, or Lionel Monckton (the latter two are composers of popular operettas).

But Mrs. Higgins recognizes that they are only thinking of Eliza as an amusement for themselves. It is fascinating to teach her and see what she can do. They are, as Mrs. Higgins says, like two babies playing with a doll. They have little consciousness of what is happening to Eliza as a person. Above all, they fail to ask themselves what sort of human being Eliza will be when they have finished their experiment. What sort of life will she be fit for? Mrs. Higgins has Mrs. Eynsford-Hill on her mind. She visualizes the possibility that Eliza may end up with the habits and tastes of a lady of leisure, without any money to live like one.

Higgins does have some grasp of what he is doing. He states that when you give a human being a new speech you are making a new person of her. He points out that this is one way to bridge the gap between social classes-and between human souls. We glimpse here Higgins' almost religious respect for his own profession.

But he does not have the imagination to apply these splendid ideas to the real-life situation. He dismisses his mother's concern easily, He does not think, as Mrs. Pearce says, He knows that he will do something for Eliza, so there is really nothing to worry about. He will find her some "light employment."

Pickering is not concerned over the matter either. He is too polite to show it clearly but he dismisses Mrs. Higgins' worries as tiresome female fuss. He reassures her politely and leaves as quickly as he can. As the two men go out, they plan to take Eliza to a Shakespeare exhibition. It will be great fun to hear her remarks and watch her imitations of the people she will see.

Mrs. Higgins is so upset by the blindness of her visitors that she cannot concentrate on her own letter writing. The scene concludes with her angry exclamation: "Oh, men! men!! men!!!"

ACT III: THE SECOND SCENE

Comment

Originally, Act III of *Pygmalion* consisted only of the first scene. Shaw stated that later on it was pointed out to him that he had omitted the "obligatory scene," the one in which Eliza finally does pass her test and Higgins wins his bet. Therefore, he wrote this scene and added it when he prepared the play for reading. The film production of *Pygmalion* included this too. We see Eliza as a brilliant success at an ambassador's reception. In the musical version of *Pygmalion, My Fair Lady*, the scene is elaborately produced; it is the conclusion and **climax** of Act I (*My Fair Lady* has two acts).

By "obligatory scene," Shaw means a scene which is so important an element of the plot that it absolutely must be shown on the stage or screen. In a sense, the scene at the grand reception is obligatory. Can we, after all, ever be satisfied with a Cinderella story if we do not see Cinderella at the ball, beautiful and triumphant? Is a scene in which Cinderella is only half a success a reasonable substitute? If this is followed by a scene in which the ball is already over, will the audience not feel cheated?

Higgins and Pickering have worked for six months to pass Eliza off as a duchess. The audience has been hearing this referred to constantly for the length of two acts. It is to be expected that we shall be allowed to see the event itself.

However, it is also possible to hold the opposite viewpoint. That is, some critics feel that Shaw was right the first time; the reception scene is not only unnecessary but undesirable. It gets in the way of the important ideas in the play.

The first act is introductory. The main action takes place in Acts II through V. Acts II and III show Eliza's external development-how she learns to be clean, well dressed, mannerly, and well spoken. The scene at Mrs. Higgin's "at-home" shows Eliza externally transformed, but with her mind and spirit still undeveloped. In Acts IV and V we see Eliza's spiritual development. At the end of the play she is an independent human being. In some ways she has advanced beyond Higgins himself.

When the play is considered in this way, the scene at the reception becomes an intrusion. It does not have any bearing on what Shaw is trying to say. To put it in is simply to provide what will be popularly successful at the cost of spoiling the fine intellectual structure of the play.

In summary, we can regard the second scene of Act III as an unnecessary afterthought on Shaw's part, or we can think of it as the most essential scene in the play.

Eliza, Higgins, and Pickering attend the ambassador's reception, dressed in splendid evening clothes; Eliza's beauty and elegance make her a sensation. Unluckily, a former pupil of Higgins is also present, a Hungarian named Nepommuck. He boasts that he can identify the background of any person by his or her speech. After conversing with Eliza, he reports that she is undoubtedly a Hungarian princess. The bet is won at last. Eliza and her two escorts leave.

Comment

The short opening dialogue between Higgins and his former pupil is highly amusing. Once again Higgins displays his complete lack of the usual social graces. He obviously dislikes the experience of being kissed on both cheeks by a bewhiskered stranger. To the stranger's question: "You remember me?" he replies "Who the devil are you?" He does not attempt to smooth matters over by suggesting that he simply cannot recall the man's name at the moment, or some excuse of that sort. After Nepommuck introduces himself, Higgins does not hesitate to ask the question that is in his mind: "Why don't you shave?"

Note: Shaw describes Nepommuck as a Pandour from Hungary. This is an armed guard attached to the nobility.

For a girl fulfilling her wildest dreams by attending a magnificent party in superb clothes and jewels, Eliza does not appear to be enjoying herself. She is quiet and tense. She walks through the reception like a somnambulist (a person walking in her sleep). Most important, she feels like an alien among the other guests. They stare at her. She senses that she is not like them and never will be. Eliza is no longer at home selling flowers on a street corner. But she is not at home as a lady of high society either.

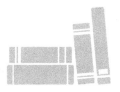

PYGMALION

ACTS 4 AND 5

. . . .

ACT IV

Eliza enters the laboratory of the house at Wimpole Street, followed by Higgins and Pickering. They have just returned home from the reception. The two men discuss the day's events, mentioning Eliza as though she were not present. Higgins is delighted that all is over; he says he has been for the past two months. The two men go upstairs to bed. As he leaves, Higgins tells Eliza to order tea for his breakfast instead of coffee. Alone, Eliza throws herself on the floor in wild, silent fury.

Comment

This scene is the best demonstration in the play of Higgins' human shortcomings. His bet has been won for him by Eliza. She has been through a grueling day, during which she has attended a garden party, a formal dinner, and an evening reception, behaving without an error the whole time. Yet he has no word of praise or thanks for her. Even the normally more considerate Pickering offers Eliza no comfort. Neither man speaks to Eliza during the entire scene, until Higgins gives her his order for breakfast as he goes out of the room.

The two men do not even bother to emphasize Eliza's accomplishment when they talk with one another about the day. Higgins speaks of the terrible boredom he has suffered all day. He could tell in three minutes that the bet was won. The remainder was hard to get through. No doubt this is praise of a sort, but it is not likely to give Eliza much satisfaction.

Higgins is happy that the whole experiment is over. It was, he states, a terrible mistake to get involved in such a tiresome project. He will never do such a thing again. Eliza listens to him thank heaven that his forced association with her is over, but she says nothing.

Higgins is full of self-pity as he reviews the experiment. He recalls the terrible nervous strain he has been through. Eliza wasn't nervous, he tells Pickering with assurance. (He does not ask her about it.)

Eliza's weariness, strain, and bitter unhappiness are brilliantly indicated in this scene, although she does not say a word until Higgins comes back into the room to get his slippers. She is a beautiful sight as she sits immobile in her evening gown and jewels, hearing Higgins discuss his boredom, hearing Pickering congratulate, not her, but Higgins on the achievement. But, striking as she is in her triumph, the men do not bother to look at her. We can feel her building up pressure inside as she sits. We are not surprised by her silent explosion.

Higgins' indifference to Eliza's everyday usefulness is also shown. He wants his slippers. Eliza brings them. He looks down a minute later and sees them. He seems to assume that they have somehow shown up by themselves. He does not notice her service, and he certainly does not thank her for it.

Higgins comes down to the laboratory again for his forgotten slippers. Eliza throws them at him. He is amazed. He demands an explanation. What is to become of her, she asks. She has been made into a creature who is not fit for any normal way of life. Higgins refuses to get excited. He suggests that she might get married, or perhaps she would rather open a florist's shop.

Eliza asks whether the clothes Pickering has bought her during the experiment actually belong to her. She returns her jewels (rented for the occasion) to Higgins so that they may be safe. She does not want to be accused of stealing, in case anything should be missing. Higgins slams out of the room, furious. Eliza, goes up to her room.

Comment

When his slippers come flying through the air at him, Higgins senses for the first time that something may be wrong with Eliza.

But even now he cannot take her problem seriously. He tries to be kind, but clearly he feels that it is his misfortune to be persecuted by the ravings of a hysterical female. Between bites of an apple, he advises Eliza to get married. (He feels that matrimony is always a possible career if a girl is unfit for anything else.) She is not bad looking, usually, he tells her kindly. Of course, she looks very ugly at the moment because she has been crying.

Eliza objects bitterly that it will be coming down in the world for her; formerly she sold flowers, but now she must sell herself. There is some suggestion in this scene that Eliza feels like a woman scorned. This is probably psychologically sound. She may have no romantic interest in Higgins; still, no woman likes it when a man who is an eligible bachelor her tells to go and find someone else to marry, with a clear implication that he would not himself apply for the role of husband under any circumstances.

This is one reason why Eliza now exercises all her ability to reduce Higgins to a state of helpless fury. She suddenly addresses him as "Sir." This indicates that she has been a servant girl all these months. She asks for permission to take her clothes. Thus, she accuses him indirectly of being mean and small-minded, which is quite unfair, since Higgins is a generous person in the material sense, whatever other faults he may have. She asks him to take charge of the jewels, to save herself from false accusations of theft, to which servants were always susceptible. Higgins has not cast any doubt on her honesty. All in all, Eliza is diabolically clever in attacking Higgins in ways that are painful to him and unfair as well. Higgins goaded by her attack. He is only conscious of how she has misinterpreted his behavior. His feelings are hurt. He relieves them by a comprehensive string of curses and goes up to his room. It does not occur to him that Eliza does really have something to complain of. He does not sense her anguish.

Eliza demonstrates her mixed feelings towards Higgins by means of the ring from Brighton. She returns to him a ring he bought her when they were at that seaside resort. He throws it angrily into the fireplace when he goes upstairs. She crawls on her hands and knees until she finds it again, for she cannot bear to leave it where he has thrown it. Yet she does not want to take it with her. She finally puts it down on a stand that holds candies and fruits. Then she too leaves the room.

ACT IV: SECOND SCENE

This is another optional scene for reading or for film production. Eliza is shown going to her room, changing her clothes, and leaving the house. Outside, she finds the lovelorn Freddy Eynsford-Hill, who spends most nights there gazing at her window. Freddy is surprised into embracing her. Lonely and unhappy, she responds. They decide to ride around in a taxi all night and then ask Mrs. Higgins' advice in the morning.

Comment

Eliza leaves the house at Wimpole Street in a wretched state. She even says to Freddy that her plan was to throw herself into the river. She has had the bruising experience of extending herself to the last extreme of her mind and nerves for Higgins' sake, only to find that he has not noticed that she has done so. He has airily passed off the strain of what she has done by saying that she was not nervous, that was she "all right."

This does not mean that Eliza has fallen in love with Higgins, or that she has expected him to fall in love with her as soon as she becomes a "lady." (However, there is always a teasing suggestion of this possibility. The question of what relationship finally comes to exists between Henry Higgins and Eliza is complex and important to an understanding of the play as a whole. It will be gone into fully later.) But it does mean that Eliza has given Higgins the greatest gift in her power-her whole-souled effort to do exactly what he has asked her to do-and has not received a "Thank you" in return.

Now as she emerges into the street she finds Freddy, not impatient like Higgins, but endlessly patient; not violent in temper, but mild and gentle; not critical of Eliza, but convinced of her absolute perfection. Above all, Freddy is full of unselfish devotion. His entire being is concentrated on Eliza. It feels wonderful to her to have somebody worship her after the way Higgins has ignored her. He has paid attention to her vowels and consonants, but as a human being he has ignored her.

Thus we may say that Eliza is caught by Freddy on the rebound. It is mainly because he is the opposite of Higgins that she responds to him.

Freddy is naively surprised that London policemen consider it their duty to chase couples who stop to kiss each other. Eliza, more worldly wise, is quite familiar with this police practice. The policemen themselves are amusing quick sketches, especially the first one who walks away, shaking his head with sad wisdom as he recalls his own courtship, and what came after!

ACT V

Mrs. Higgins' parlourmaid informs her that her son and Colonel Pickering are in the house. They are telephoning the police. Mrs. Higgins sends word to Eliza to stay upstairs out of sight until Mrs. Higgins sends for her. Higgins enters the room in a state of great excitement and announces that Eliza is missing.

Comment

The mood and action of the scene are most skillfully foreshadowed in the brief opening exchange between Mrs. Higgins and the maid. We learn that Higgins is "in a state." He is sufficiently upset to be telephoning the police. As his mother amusingly puts it, he has lost something. A piece of his property has disappeared. It might be a wallet he is reporting missing; it might be a dog; but as it happens, it is Eliza that is missing.

Mrs. Higgins also makes it clear to us that Eliza has come to her house for refuge and advice, just as she intended to do at the end of Act IV.

When Higgins enters, he is so full of his grievance that he neglects to say "Good morning" to his mother before he tells her about it. Gently but firmly, she makes him correct this. It is characteristic of her that she always insists on formal courtesy, no matter what the situation. This is probably because she remains in a calm state of mind when other people get excited and forget themselves.

Mrs. Higgins suggests tentatively that something must be wrong for Eliza to run away, but Higgins is still unable to grasp this. He calls it nonsense. What is bothering him is that all this is an inconvenience; Eliza has been taking care of his possessions and his appointments, and this morning he is suffering from her absence.

The conversation is interrupted by the arrival of Alfred Doolittle. He is magnificently dressed, from his top hat to his patent leather shoes. He is furious at Higgins, for Higgins once mentioned in a letter to an American millionaire that Doolittle was the most original moralist in England, with the result that the millionaire has left Doolittle pounds 4,000 ($20,000) a year in his will. Thus Doolittle is no longer one of the happy Undeserving Poor; he is middle-class. Mrs. Higgins sees a silver lining in the situation-he will be able to support Eliza. Higgins objects angrily to this, for he feels Eliza belongs to him. Doolittle objects too.

Comment

The arrival of Eliza's unspeakable parent, who has been absent since an early point in the play, once again adds variety and diversion to the action. We are astonished at Doolittle's prosperous appearance. The Eliza-Higgins relationship is forgotten temporarily as we are diverted by the strange rise of Alfred Doolittle. As a result of a joke by Higgins in a letter, a moral-minded American millionaire (who could not have had much sense of humor) has made Doolittle almost rich, for even today $20,000 is a substantial yearly income, and in 1912 it had several times the purchasing power it has now. (The millionaire's name is Ezra D. Wannafeller. "Wannafeller" is of course a combination of "Wanamaker," the great American merchant family, and "Rockefeller," an American family that requires no introduction to the reader. For some reason, many European writers, including Shaw, have had the mistaken idea that "Ezra" is a very common first name in modern America.)

The best part of the joke is the contrast between Doolittle in Act II and the same man in Act V. The disreputable trash collector of the second act was a happy man. He praised the life he lived as one of the Undeserving Poor. He departed with satisfaction after selling his rights in Eliza for five pounds. But this Doolittle, clean, well-dressed, and respectable, complains bitterly against the fate that has pushed him into the middle-class against his will. He looks back on his poor days as the time of lost happiness.

With gloomy relish, Doolittle lists the many disadvantages of his new status. Everyone has some service to sell him now. His solicitor (lawyer) is delighted at Doolittle's good fortune, because it means business for him. Doctors who would scarcely have bothered with him as a charity patient suddenly find he is in poor health and needs constant care. He must pay servants in his home to do the things he would rather do himself. And suddenly he has fifty relatives, none of them able to earn his own living. Eliza too will probably expect him to support her. Even Henry Higgins will soon be taking money from him, for he will have to learn to speak "middle-class language" instead of his own comfortable slum dialect, which he calls "proper English."

Doolittle has even been robbed of his courage by the millionaire's money. When Henry Higgins wanted to give him ten pounds instead of five at their first meeting, he steadfastly refused the extra five because so much money might make him cautious. But Doolittle cannot find the strength to refuse four thousand pounds. If he does not accept it, he must face old age as a pauper in the workhouse.

Note: Doolittle speaks of being caught between "Skilly" and "Char Bydis." He means "Scylla" and "Charybdis". These are great rock on the Italian coast and a whirlpool near the coast of Sicily. They are represented as two sea monsters by the ancient Greek poet Homer. To be caught between Scylla and Charybdis is to be caught between two terrible alternatives.

Mrs. Higgins now tells her son that Eliza is in the house. She explains to him and to Pickering why their conduct was thoughtless and unfeeling toward Eliza. At Mrs. Higgins' suggestion, Mr. Doolittle waits out on the balcony as Eliza comes to confront her two teachers. Eliza is calm and gracious. She is coolly polite to Higgins but really warm in her thanks to Pickering. However, she states firmly that she will never return to Wimpole Street.

Comment

As Mrs. Higgins explains in words of one syllable why Eliza has left the house on Wimpole Street, Pickering understands at last and is ashamed. But not Higgins. Before his mother's explanation, Higgins gives his version of what happened after Pickering left the laboratory the night before. It seems that Eliza made an outrageous, unprovoked attack on him with the slippers. He didn't say a word, and she threw them at him the moment he came into the room. He does not change this interpretation during the scene. He sees himself as Eliza's victim. Higgins' anger is increased when Eliza behaves with elegant courtesy toward him and Pickering. After all, he taught her to behave like this, and now she is turning his teaching against him.

This interpretation by Higgins is most important. It shows that he has not grasped what has happened to Eliza. He roars that she will relapse into the gutter without him to direct her. He calls her a "thing" that he has created out of squashed cabbage leaves.

But Eliza is a transformed human being. Somehow, as she has acquired new speech and new manners, she has acquired also a new kind of humanity. She has been changed in her soul. She is something beyond Higgins' creation. She has abilities that Higgins never gave her. It is not only that she is now a match for Higgins, that she can reduce him to a fuming rage without getting excited herself. It is also her awareness of the part Pickering has played in her development. She thanks him for his generosity towards her. But she thanks him even more his ever-present good manners. The new Eliza understands that the difference between a lady and a flower girl is not how she acts, but how people act towards her.

Some critics have thought that it is more accurate to think of Pickering as the Pygmalion of the title than Higgins. After all, it is Pickering who first recognizes and responds to Eliza's innocence and courage. It is Pickering who calls her "Miss Doolittle," which she regards as a milestone in her transformation. It is Pickering's courtesy that literally makes a lady out of her, as she carefully explains. Compared to all this, Higgin's contribution is unimportant.

However, if we read the preface to the play with care, we cannot escape the fact that it is a transformation through phonetics that Shaw is referring to in this play. The concluding essay also bears this out, for here Shaw refers to Higgins and Eliza as Pygmalion and Galatea. Thus, though Pickering's part in Eliza's growth is of very great importance, there is no doubt that Higgins' work is more important as Shaw sees it. Bad speech is a badge of class limitation. Once it disappears, all else becomes possible.

In this scene, we are again treated to the sight of Mrs. Higgins' controlling her son's unmannerliness with weary patience. She makes him sit up straight. She forces him to stop whistling. She tries to control his behavior toward Eliza. She reproaches him for swearing when Eliza asks that he call her Miss Doolittle. She also suggests that if he cannot behave himself he should please go home, since he has taken up a great deal of her time. This is refreshingly unlike the attitude of most doting mothers.

To summarize, the complex relationship among Eliza, Higgins, and Pickering again takes the center of the stage. Eliza is shown as an exceptional human being, far more than the creation of Higgins' phonetic training. Higgins cannot grasp this yet. He still treats Eliza as an ignorant flower girl with improved speech. Pickering begins to understand what is happening.

Eliza is just saying that she will never again make one of her old sounds when her father appears without warning. She lets out a terrible noise straight from her old life, to Higgins' great satisfaction. Doolittle reveals that he is about to marry Eliza's "step-mother,"-another painful result of middle-class morality. Eliza agrees to attend the wedding. She goes to get her hat and returns quickly. Pickering will attend Doolittle as best man. Mrs. Higgins will be a wedding guest. Doolittle and Pickering leave for the church. Mrs. Higgins goes to get ready. Higgins and Eliza are left alone.

Comment

The purpose of all this elaborate bustling around is of course to get rid of the other characters so that Higgins and Eliza may be left alone to confront one another. It is not easy for a playwright to dispose of three characters in a natural manner, for it is a harder task to get characters off the stage when the writer is finished with them than it is to get them on the scene in the first place. Shaw has great technical ability at solving such dramatic problems. He has Eliza get ready for the wedding first, so that she has no reason to leave the room. Pickering and the condemned bridegroom naturally depart early. Mrs. Higgins has arrangements to make, for she has had no knowledge that she would be attending a wedding on this day. Thus, Shaw's purpose is accomplished. The vital scene between Higgins and Eliza can begin.

Eliza and Higgins now talk out their relationship. Higgins sometimes cajoles her and sometimes abuses her. He wants her to return to his house. He admits that he would miss her if he should not see her any more. But he will not make the concession that Eliza wants; he will not promise to treat her politely and considerately. He treats her the same as he treats everybody else. He refuses to treat her any better.

Eliza does not mind being treated rudely. But she does mind being ignored. She cannot endure the fact that Higgins has no real feeling for her. She says she does not want Higgins to be in love with her, but she does want him to have some human regard for her. She says she will earn her living as a teacher of phonetics and marry Freddy as soon as she can support him. Higgins is in a rage, but he is baffled. As the play ends, Eliza goes out with Mrs. Higgins, leaving Higgins laughing contemptuously as he thinks of Eliza marrying Freddy.

Comment

This concluding dialogue between Higgins and Eliza is masterly and complex. It has a quality which is to be found in almost all great drama; the dialogue says not only what is in the lines, but a good deal more. There are overtones and undertones. There are subtleties of character. There is a clash of ideas, but there is also an emotional communication which breathes through the intellectual content. In Higgins' case especially, we sense that he is not only trying to get Eliza to come back on his own terms, but that he is making a desperate fight against a situation that threatens to control him.

Eliza is in full scale revolt against her position in Higgins' world. She does not mind fetching and carrying, doing his errands, remembering his appointments. She does not even mind, she says, when he is abusive in his language. But she does mind being only an element of convenience. She cannot endure it when she has no existence, no human individuality, where he is concerned. After the great reception, when she saw that she was only a part of a problem solved, she was shattered. She cannot live any longer on those terms. In fact, she will not.

Higgins now works to make Eliza return to Wimpole Street. He uses all his charm, which is considerable. It works very well on Mrs. Pearce, who stays in Higgins' employ against her better judgment. It is usually quite effective with women when he bothers to use it (with the exception of his mother). He coaxes and soothes her. He even goes so far as to admit that her voice and appearance are pleasing to him.

But he is impatient when she does not respond at once. Also, he will not go beyond a certain point in his efforts to make up with her. He will not agree to be careful of her feelings. He will not state that he has any feeling for her. The most he will say is that she is a part of humanity that he has "built into my house."

Higgins bluntly values his work more than Eliza. He made her a duchess because he was doing his job. He did not stop to consider what might happen to her, because he is more interested in doing his work than in avoiding trouble for her or for himself.

Higgins is enraged when Eliza speaks of offering her services to Nepommuck. Yet, he now finds Eliza admirable as a person who can act quite independently of him. She is a "consort battleship." She can return to Wimpole Street as an equal.

The conversation ends inconclusively. Questions arise in the reader's mind. Perhaps the most basic ones are: What does Eliza really want from Higgins? Why is Higgins anxious for Eliza's return? What does Higgins really want from Eliza? Eliza emphasizes constantly Higgins' lack of feeling for her. She says he does not care a bit for her. She refuses to care for anybody who does not care for her. She asks him why he transformed her if he did not care for her. Surely Eliza is saying in effect: "Tell me that I mean something to you. Tell me how you need me." Notice too that when Higgins suggests that she marry Pickering, she flashes back: "I wouldn't marry you if you asked me." He has not mentioned any such idea.

Freddy is Eliza's best weapon. She tells Higgins about the many letters Freddy sends her. His annoyance is most encouraging to her. Near the end of their talk, she says she will marry Freddy. Higgins roars his disgust; Freddy is not worthy of her!

When we put together all these indications we see that Eliza's anger is in reality a way of pleading. She wants to know that Higgins loves and needs her-that he can at least think of marrying her. She even goes so far as to say that while they worked together she came to care for Higgins-not in a passionate way, but "more friendly like."

Higgins is a man who wants something but desperately tries to avoid paying the usual price. He wants Eliza back. He wants this woman in his house. He wants her to help run his home and his life. He wants the comfort of her companionship. But if he can, he wants to get all this without paying the price of personal surrender. He does not want Eliza as a wife. He wants to belong to himself and go to his own way just as before.

His efforts to accomplish this are ludicrous. His compliments to Eliza are determinedly non-romantic. He calls her a "consort battleship." He says that he, she and Pickering will be three old bachelors together-surely one of the most peculiar compliments a girl has ever received.

Higgins is for the first time a little pathetic as he fights against his feelings for the sake of a future in which everything will be unchanged and under his own control.

The outcome is left in doubt. Perhaps Higgins will be saved by his desperate struggle. With the help of his Oedipus complex and his bad manners, he may escape from the net that he feels closing around him. Perhaps Eliza will understand that in answer to her question: "Do you want me?" Higgins can only say: "Yes, in a way, but-" She may prefer Freddy to that.

The play *Pygmalion* is distinguished rather than run-of-the-mill precisely because its ending is ambiguous. If it ended with Eliza in Higgins' arms, it would be a delightful comedy which follows a well-worn path to an expected conclusion. As it is, it leaves the reader or audience alert and stimulated.

THE CONCLUDING ESSAY

Shaw explains what happened to the characters in the play. Eliza did not marry Higgins. He was too attached to his mother and to his work. She could never come first with him. Eliza married Freddy. With the financial aid of Colonel Pickering, they set up a florist's shop. After early troubles caused by their inexperience, the shop prospered. Eliza remained close to Higgins and Pickering, although she always fought back vigorously when Higgins tried to bully her.

The fate of two secondary characters is also made clear. Alfred Doolittle became a success with the highest social classes. Clara, Freddy's sister, read the novels of H. G. Wells, became converted to Socialism, and got a job instead of living in discontented idleness.

Comment

This essay was added to the original play by Shaw after the first London production, which was produced by a famous actor of the day, Sir Herbert Beerbohm Tree, who also performed the part of Henry Higgins. Shaw was extremely irritated by Tree, who did everything he could to destroy the final ambiguity about Higgins and Eliza that Shaw had so carefully created. Tree was unable to understand what Shaw had in mind; he played Higgins as a romantic hero.

Shaw fought with Tree all during rehearsals, trying to maintain the original emphasis of the play. On opening night, Tree threw a bouquet of flowers to Eliza as she went downstairs to go to her father's wedding, just before the curtain came down. With this single gesture, he managed to destroy the meaning of Act V.

Shaw's response was to write this essay, stating flatly that Eliza married Freddy and not Higgins. Of course, in counteracting Tree's unwise performance, he also unbalanced the beautiful subtlety of the last act of his play.

Eliza, Freddy, and Higgins. Shaw makes a good case for Eliza's choice of Freddy as a husband (which is left as a possibility in the play). Higgins is closely bound to his mother. He cares about his work more than he could ever care about any woman. And he is domineering. Eliza is a strong personality herself; she cannot accept Higgins' bullying. Freddy is dependent on her, but he loves her. Like many strong people, Eliza chooses a mate weaker than herself.

Shaw's final point is that Eliza is in a sense Higgins' creation. He is almost godlike to her. Galatea cannot really like Pygmalion; the nature of their relationship prevents it.

Clara and H. G. Wells. Shaw gives a very realistic description of a change in Clara's way of living and thinking. He states that this began with her reading of the novels of H. G. Wells and came to a **climax** when she managed to meet Wells himself at a party.

H. G. Wells is, of course a real person whom Shaw introduces, in the final essay, to one of the imaginary characters of the play. The effect is amusing. Wells and Shaw knew each other intimately. Wells was a prolific novelist. He wrote a number of science fiction novels such as *The Invisible Man* and *The War of the Worlds*, but his reputation as an important novelist rests on *Kipps*, *The History of Mr. Polly*, and several other realistic novels of English middle-class life. The novels express Wells' hatred of Victorian ideas and his sympathy with Socialist reforms.

Shaw invents a meeting between Clara and Wells at a garden party. Clara is tremendously impressed. As Shaw wittily puts it: "Age had not withered him, nor could custom stale his infinite variety in half an hour." (This is a paraphrase of a famous description of Cleopatra in Shakespeare's *Anthony and Cleopatra*: "Age could not wither nor custom stale / Her infinite variety." Shaw adds a deflating touch to it: Wells is apparently infinitely varied enough to be fascinating for half an hour, at least.

Clara talks constantly of her meeting with Wells. At last, an acquaintance offers her a job in a furniture shop on the chance that Clara may be able to bring Wells to the shop. Thus, finally both the young Eynsford-Hills are sensibly occupied in making a living, instead of trying to live a life of elegant leisure for which they do not have the money.

We should note that the idea of an essay like this, which ties up all loose ends in the play but cannot possibly be represented on a stage, would not occur to most dramatists. Shaw can make use of it because he always feels that his plays are as much to be read as to be performed. This is only one of many things he includes primarily for the pleasure of the reader. Others are the prefaces to various plays and the lengthy descriptions of the characters.

PYGMALION

. . . .

HENRY HIGGINS

Higgins' portrait is based to some extent on real-life models. One was the famous phonetics specialist Henry Sweet, a man still revered as one of the great figures in his field. Like Higgins, Sweet was short-tempered, eccentric, and completely devoted to his work. The other model was Robert Bridges, a famous poet and student of language with a special interest in the writings of John Milton, the English poet. Higgins too is deeply influenced by Milton.

Higgins' most attractive characteristic is a certain innocence which is in contrast to his professional skill and intellectual sophistication. He causes much trouble to the people who come into contact with him-Eliza, Mrs. Pearce, Mrs. Higgins-but he has no intention of hurting anybody. He is neither cruel nor mean. He treats everyone fairly and decently according to his own standards. His responses to any situation are direct and immediate, and usually loud. He simply does not give much thought to people's feelings.

Higgins' own picture of himself is as an exceptionally amiable, mild, kindly man who is often victimized by the unreasonable behavior of other people. His good intentions, as well as his comically inaccurate idea of his own nature, make him consistently appealing.

But in actuality, Higgins likes to get his own way. When an idea seizes him, as in <u>Act II</u>, he rides roughshod over all opposition. He does not care for Pickering's doubts, nor for Mrs. Pearce's disapproval, nor for Eliza's ignorant terror. He tries to placate Mrs. Pearce by offering her a daughter to adopt (not asking her whether she wants one, nor asking Eliza whether she wants to be one). He weaves wild fantasies of rich marriages to tempt Eliza. He is as irresponsible as a child who will do anything to get its hands on a new toy.

Higgins is completely devoted to his work. He has an exalted view of its spiritual importance. He is one of the guardians of the language of Shakespeare and Milton. He opens this mighty treasure to share with his pupils and thus ennobles their souls and frees them from the restraints of artificial class barriers.

This devotion is one of the things that help to make him such a terror. His work is of vital significance; other things are so trivial compared to it that they are a waste of time. Thus he will not bother with manners, social small talk, or the other amenities of civilized living. As a result, he is a trial to his mother. The repeated display of Higgin's bad manners is one of the comic elements of the play. He is especially funny in his outspoken honesty at times where polite lying is the usual behavior. During his mother's "at home" in Act III, he greets Mrs. Eynsford-Hill and her daughter gloomily, unable to pretend that he is glad to see them. The arrival of Freddy is the last straw.

Higgins groans: "God of Heaven! another of them." It is no wonder that his mother wishes he would stay in his own house when she is having guests.

Higgins swears constantly. Mrs. Pearce puts up with his language in martyred patience. Even Colonel Pickering, who is an Army man, after all, and accustomed to such things, mentions that he has seldom heard anything like it.

Personal untidiness is another of Higgin's characteristics. He uses his dressing gown to wipe his hands on at meals. He shoves all his food onto the same plate. Mrs. Pearce mentions these matters during the amusing scene in Act II when she lectures him about improving his manners as an example to Eliza. At that time she points out that he nearly choked recently on a fish bone in the jam jar, a bone he must have dropped into the jar himself. Eliza herself points out in Act V that, if it were not for Colonel Pickering, she would never have known how ladies and gentlemen behave. She mentions particularly Higgins' habit of taking off his shoes in the dining room.

Towards Eliza, Higgins is domineering and impatient. He becomes absorbed in her as an object involved in a phonetics experiment. It turns out that Eliza is a woman with exceptional qualities of mind and heart. He senses that he has allowed himself to come to the brink of a truly profound human relationship. He fights hard to retain for himself the pleasure and convenience of Eliza's presence without making any further gift of himself to her. He does not want to change his ways or belong to anybody but himself. At the end of the play we are left uncertain about the outcome of this interior struggle.

ELIZA DOOLITTLE

When we first see Eliza, she is a child of the London streets, dirty, shabby, ignorant, and accustomed to standing up for her own rights, since there is nobody else to do it for her. For instance, she is almost ready to quarrel with the Eynsford-Hills over payment for the flowers Freddy has accidentally spoiled. She is quite persistent as she tries to persuade Colonel Pickering to buy a flower from her. She puts up a great howl of protest against the "policeman" (really Higgins) who is writing down her words.

But her ignorance is so great that she gives the impression of being slightly stupid. She is sure that she is about to be arrested because she has addressed Colonel Pickering as "captain", and it is very difficult to persuade her that this whole idea is absurd.

Her ignorance has its comic side. She has never seen a bathtub. When she does, she refuses to use it because she feels it is both dangerous and indecent to take off all one's clothes and get wet all over; she knows of someone who did it every Saturday night and died from it! Mrs. Pearce gets her into the tub by a combination of force and trickery.

Eliza does have standards of behavior. She does not drink. She is "a good girl," she insists, and she is convincing. We are sure that this is true; we feel admiration for the young girl who was turned out by her father and stepmother because she was big enough to look after herself, and who has managed to stay sober and self-respecting in the midst of extreme poverty. Eliza is only eighteen or twenty when the play begins. She may have been a good deal younger when she was first forced to make her own living.

The revelation of Eliza's possibilities begins with her external self and progresses until we see the qualities of her spirit-qualities which might have stayed hidden all her life if it were not for Higgins and Pickering. A bath reveals that Eliza is attractive. A few good clothes show that she is also capable of being stylish and distinguished. Some hard work by Higgins shows that she has a sharp ear for sound and speech. Soon she can pronounce her native tongue better than most people.

But to uncover the possibilities of Eliza's mind is a much harder thing. In Mrs. Higgins' drawing room, Eliza still displays the mind of a girl brought up in a squalid world of drunkenness and violence. This contrast between her refined dress and **diction** on the one hand, and the content of her conversation on the other is what makes the high comedy of the scene. It also pitiful as it reveals that Eliza's background is still very much with her. Finally, it shows that much inner development will be necessary. By the end of the play, Eliza has become a different person inside as well as outside. She is able to analyze her own situation. She can move beautifully through the world of garden parties and receptions, but she does not really belong in that world. The other guests sense this as well as she does. They look upon her as a beautiful but alien visitor, not as one of themselves. Yet she is no longer able to return to the world she came from. Dirt and rags and flower baskets no longer constitute a possible way of life for her. She cannot see where she belongs. Hence her anguished cry: "What's o become of me?"

The only emotional haven she has is the life she has built with Higgins and Pickering. But as she hears the discussion of how boring the experiment has been to Higgins, that refuge fades away. She is sure that Higgins does not want her and cannot wait to be rid of her. In this, as it happens, she is wrong.

But she courageously acts on her understanding of what is going on; she leaves.

The shock of leaving the Wimpole Street house and going off on her own again changes Eliza's perspective. She is able to call upon her own dignity and self-sufficiency as she meets with Higgins. She tries to discover definitely how he feels about her, and whether her going has shocked his selfish mind into sympathy or appreciation. Here too she shows her appreciation of all that Colonel Pickering has done for her. She is also able to evaluate Freddy Eynsford-Hill. She sees his weaknesses but also understands the desirable qualities he offers as a husband.

Thus, with warm intuition and a capable brain, Eliza is able to analyze the men who are the factors in her life at the moment. We leave her considering the splendid and exasperating qualities of Higgins, and the unremarkable but comforting qualities of the adoring Freddy. She says she will marry Freddy, but we are not sure.

We should note also that by the end of the play Eliza has come to understand Higgins well enough to make him thoroughly uncomfortable when she wants to. She quarrels with him far more cleverly than he does with her. His outbreaks are noisy but blundering and innocent. She makes him squirm quite deliberately. She will never be able to cope with that difficult man completely, but she is not helpless at his hands any longer.

COLONEL PICKERING

Pickering is the opposite of Higgins in almost every way. The two men are alike mainly in their interest in phonetics. Pickering is courteous, while Higgins is ill-mannered. He is patient while

Higgins is brusque. He is even-tempered, but Higgins has an explosive disposition. Pickering is kindly in his impulses, while Higgins is sometimes mischievous and often thoughtless.

Eliza feels much gratitude toward Pickering, and properly so. He gives generous financial help. But, more important, he gives that courteous consideration by which she learns about being a lady. Eliza's outlook changes from the moment that Pickering calls her "Miss Doolittle" and offers her a seat. As she intelligently explains it later on: "The difference between a lady and a flower girl is not how she behaves, but how she is treated."

Pickering is also capable of showing a certain shortsightedness. Along with Higgins, he is distinctly impatient as Higgins' mother urges them to take some thought for Eliza's future. He is too amused by Eliza's progress to think about this important subject. Pickering's considerateness deserts him for a short time after Eliza's great triumph. He can do nothing but talk about his own feelings and congratulate Higgins. He has no word of praise or reassurance for Eliza.

But on the whole, Pickering personifies sanity and conventional behavior in the play. This points up Higgins' eccentricity. It should be added that Pickering is not a dithering fool and should not be played that way, though he often is.

ALFRED DOOLITTLE

Eliza's father does not have any vital part in the action of the play, but we always greet his arrival on the stage with great pleasure. He is an extraordinary man whose highly colored personality adds a vivid touch to the scenes he appears in.

Doolittle is a scoundrel. He is an exceptional scoundrel in two ways. First he is genuinely honest about it. He makes no pretense of virtue whatever. He has no morals, he admits cheerfully. He can't afford them. He talks Higgins out of five pounds in payment for Eliza. He feels that if Eliza has sold herself into a life of dishonor, he ought to get a small percentage of the proceeds. Higgins and Pickering are scandalized at this conduct, but they are so delighted with Doolittle's amiable eloquence that they end up offering him ten pounds instead of five.

Second, Doolittle is a philosophical rogue. He has given some thought to the world and his own place in it. Thus, the life he leads is the result of careful consideration. He is, he explains, one of the Undeserving Poor. The Deserving Poor sometimes receive charity, but the Undeserving Poor never do. This is most unreasonable, for his expenses are higher than those of the Deserving Poor. He has to spend a lot on liquor, for instance. However, he has become one of the Undeserving Poor because he likes it, and he plans to remain one.

Doolittle expresses his views in rich, musical speech. Higgins ascribes his eloquence to the fact that his mother was Welsh. He also makes constant use of paradox and unexpected turns of thought. For example, when Pickering expresses fear that he will put the five pounds to bad use, Doolittle reassures him: he will not save it and thus avoid working, but will use it all for an enormous spree. The spree is, of course, just what Pickering is afraid of.

The higher Doolittle rises in the world, the more unhappy he becomes. He is embittered because he has been left four thousand pounds a year by an American millionaire. Respectability has been thrust upon him. He is a prisoner of middle-class morality.

He is even going to marry Eliza's stepmother, as his gorgeous formal clothes testify.

The worst of his prosperity is that he does not have the courage to refuse it. Though surrounded by lawyers, doctors, and servants eager to provide their services for a fat fee, though preyed on by impecunious relatives, Doolittle cannot quite face the prospect of giving it all up, because the alternative for him is inevitably the workhouse (poorhouse) in his old age, which is fast approaching.

The last time we see Doolittle, as he departs for his own wedding, he is a miserable man.

MRS. HIGGINS

Mrs. Higgins inspires great devotion in her son. She is a handsome, elegant woman who lives a well-regulated life. She obviously has artistic interests. Her home is furnished in splendid taste. It reflects the best and most advanced artistic thought of her own youth. The arrival of her eccentric son almost always means a disruption in Mrs. Higgins' orderly, pleasant existence. He upsets her house, breaks her furniture, and insults her friends. She is consequently distressed if he arrives unexpectedly.

We note from this that Mrs. Higgins does not show a possessive, smothering attitude towards her son. She is clearly fond of him, but she is also pleased that their lives move on separate paths. If Higgins is exceptionally attached to his mother, as he says, it is not because she ties him to her apron strings.

Mrs. Higgins is a perceptive person. She understands immediately the fascination her son feels for his experiment with Eliza. She recognizes the danger of the situation. However, she cannot make this clear to her son or to Pickering. They cheerfully assure her that there is nothing to worry about.

When Eliza comes to Mrs. Higgins in her distress, she is treated with sympathy. Mrs. Higgins tries to help her by explaining to Higgins what he has done to Eliza. Mrs. Higgins also shows her instinctive kindness and perfect courtesy earlier in the play. She does all she can to make Eliza feel welcome when Higgins brings her to visit.

MRS. PEARCE

Mrs. Pearce appears only in Act II, though she is referred to later in the play more than once. She adds an extra dimension of humor. Like Pickering, she is sane and normal, and she thus provides an excellent balance for Higgins' eccentricity. While Pickering is a "gentleman," that is, a person of excellent social background who has been to the best English public schools, Mrs. Pearce is very much a middle-class person. She has definite and somewhat narrow ideas of what is right and wrong. She is rigidly respectable. Added to this are common sense and practical intelligence. She is immediately aware of all the problems that must be dealt with if Eliza is to stay at Wimpole Street and be taught by Higgins. Is she married? What about her parents? Will she be paid a salary? What is her exact status in the household to be?

Mrs. Pearce has a strong character. She is used to Higgins' coaxing ways when he wants something. She is unyielding when she feels that a principle is at stake. She behaves toward her employer almost as though she were a governess or teacher and he were a difficult little boy. She is unfailingly courteous but quite firm as she discusses Higgins' bad manners and bad language and the necessity of improving both as an example to Eliza. Higgins' extravagance and Mrs. Pearce's primness make an amusing contrast. We can share Pickering's enjoyment of their discussion.

Mrs. Pearce's unwillingness to repeat the word "bloody" is another indication of her rigidly decent middle-class standards.

There is no softness about Mrs. Pearce, but she does not lack kindness either. She understands Eliza's terror over Higgins' wild conversation; she interprets his talk and tries to reassure her. Like Mrs. Higgins, Mrs. Pearce has genuine concern for Eliza's future.

MRS. EYNSFORD-HILL

Mrs. Eynsford-Hill is a rather conservative lady of kindly instincts who has been brought up to lead a life of aristocratic idleness. Unfortunately, she does not possess an aristocratic income. She is forbidden by all the traditions of her social class to get a job or to let her children get jobs. Therefore, she struggles along on a pitiful amount of money, constantly worried over finances and concerned over the future of her two children.

CLARA EYNSFORD-HILL

Without any legitimate outlet for her energy or ability, Clara Eynsford-Hill idles away her life in what Colonel Pickering calls "the social routine." However, her social opportunities are limited because she has little money. Thus, while all her efforts are directed at her social life, she often has the unhappy feeling that she is not in the midst of what is going on. She wants to be up-to-date. But she is never sure that she is succeeding. This insecurity makes it easy for Higgins to persuade her to say the disagreeably vulgar word "bloody" under the impression that it is the newest slang. The circumstances of her life make Clara fretful and unpleasant. In the essay which he wrote after the play was produced, Shaw traces Clara's later destiny. He describes how she was converted to modern social ideas by the novels of H. G. Wells, and how she finally got a job and supported herself. Though she remained an aggressive person, her personality was much improved by these events.

FREDDY EYNSFORD-HILL

Freddy is more agreeable than his sister. However, he shows little evidence of ability or brains. In fact, he is so amiably ineffectual that he may remind the reader of those idiotic young men who later became a specialty of P. G. Wodehouse in his numerous comic novels.

Eliza is attracted to his good looks, gentlemanly behavior, and good nature. Most of all, she is touched because of his complete devotion to her. Whether all this is enough to counterbalance the more colorful attractiveness of Professor Higgins is left unsettled in the play. The final essay states that Freddy and Eliza marry.

PYGMALION

Question: What is the science of phonetics? What is its practical importance in the play? What is its symbolic importance?

Answer: Phonetics concerns the sounds of human speech, particularly how they are produced and how they may be classified. This subject had an extremely rapid development in the nineteenth century. One of its pioneers was Henry Sweet, the cantankerous Oxford scholar who was one of the models for Shaw's portrait of Higgins. Sweet was an inventor (though not the only one) of the International Phonetic Alphabet. This made it possible to record human speech precisely, which could not be done with the conventional alphabet. In the play Higgins is the inventor of a fictional phonetic alphabet named Higgins' Universal Alphabet.

Shaw took delight in writing *Pygmalion* because he was thus able to show that what seemed like a dry, unpromising subject could be turned into a lively play. This was done by making clear the practical implications of phonetics. By means of it, a person's speech could be changed. With the change in speech, a change in life was possible. By developing the idea of this change, Shaw developed the play.

Thus, a familiar and enjoyable story is retold. It is the story of Galatea, as the title suggests. It is also the story of Cinderella. Only here the chief force is not magic, but the expert ability of Higgins. The change includes dramatic alterations in cleanliness, manners, and dress, but the original and most important element is the change in speech.

The change in speech also has symbolic value. The difference between cultivated and unacceptable speech is one of the chief symbols of the difference between social classes. This difference has been for most people unchangeable. The speech with which most human beings grow up is the speech they keep all their lives. It marks them unmistakably. Here Higgins, and through him Shaw, shows that this great difference between human beings can be destroyed. And when this disappears, the class distinction it represents also largely disappears. The flower girl does not have to stay on the curbstone with her basket all her life. To re-make human speech is a method of re-making modern society.

Question: Explain the importance of Colonel Pickering in the development of the play.

Answer: Pickering's role in *Pygmalion* is inconspicuous, but it is not unimportant. Note that he is present almost constantly throughout the play, often playing an important part. It is he who sets the machinery of the play going and keeps it in motion. His curiosity about what Higgins is doing in the opening scene prompts Higgins' explanation about phonetics and the importance of human speech. Eliza overhears this; therefore she arrives at Wimpole Street the next day to buy lessons for a shilling each. Here again Pickering reminds Higgins of his boast of the previous night. He offers a bet that Higgins cannot make a duchess of the flower girl within six months. This plunges Higgins into his "inspired folly"; he accepts the bet and the main action of the play proceeds, with Pickering paying the bills for Eliza's transformation.

Pickering himself has much to do with the change in Eliza. From the first day she comes to Wimpole Street he treats her with the kindly courtesy that is so natural to him. When Higgins and Mrs. Pearce order Eliza to sit down, she refuses to do so, half-rebellious, half-afraid. Pickering quietly invites her to do so, addressing her as "Miss Doolittle." She takes the offered chair at once.

In Act V, Eliza expresses her great obligation to Pickering, remarking that it was from him that she learned how ladies and gentlemen behave. She dates her education from the moment Pickering first called her "Miss Doolittle." In fact, she tends to dismiss Higgins' contribution lightly; she simply took lessons from him in his professional capacity, as she might learn to dance from a dancing teacher. For this reason, it has been suggested that Pickering is the Pygmalion of the story, not Higgins. However, the whole substance of the play, including the preface and the final essay, weighs heavily against this idea.

Shaw also uses Pickering as a contrast to Higgins. This serves to bring out Higgins' characteristics more sharply. Where Higgins is noisy, short-tempered, imaginative, willful, unmannerly, and somewhat immature in the area of human relations, Pickering is quiet, patient, reasonable, courteous, and kind. He too has his weaknesses, of course. His interest in the experiment causes him to forget the necessity of keeping Eliza's future in mind.

And, like Higgins, he does not bother to congratulate Eliza after her triumph.

To summarize, Pickering is important to the structure of the play because he causes the main action to take place. His good treatment of Eliza is an important cause of the change in her. And his conventional personality is an effective contrast to Higgins' more colorful one.

Question: Analyze Shaw's method of portraying Higgins. How does he make him attractive in spite of his weaknesses?

Answer: Henry Higgins, as Shaw portrays him, has many characteristics that we would find unattractive if we were to meet them in real people. He is rude and inconsiderate, even to harmless strangers like the Eynsford-Hills, when he meets them in his mother's drawing room. He acts as if other people have no feelings. Note the way he talks about Eliza in Act II; he suggests that she will drink if given money, and he pays no attention to her vigorous protests, not to those of Pickering.

He is ruthless about getting his way, whether he has to do it by giving an exhibition of bad temper of by wheedling and coaxing. When he wants Eliza for his experiment, no obstacle stops him.

Yet, in his description of Higgins, Shaw says that he remains likeable at all times. Furthermore, this is actually so. Higgins is appealing throughout the play, even when his ignorance of human feelings causes us to pity Eliza and feel angry at him. This shows that Shaw has excellent control over his dramatic materials.

The main reason that Higgins remains appealing is that he means no harm. He is not vicious nor cruel. His intentions are never bad, even when his behavior is most unreasonable. Also, he himself does not realize how unreasonable he sometimes is. He sees himself as the mildest, most patient of men, who is constantly having to struggle with stupid people and bad circumstances.

Thus, there is a sort of innocence about his tantrums. He does not see that he rides roughshod over other people. Besides this, Shaw makes his bad temper and bad manners so extravagant that they are comical. His rudeness at his mother's "at home" is an example of this.

We are also sympathetic to Higgins because he is undeveloped in certain ways. When he finds that Eliza has become important to him, his struggles are pitiable. He has no real understanding of what has happened to him. He only knows instinctively that the way of life he has created is now threatened. He cannot easily free himself from her. Nor can he give up the comfort of his independence. Most of us feel we are no match for Higgins in intellectual force. Yet most of us are more understanding than he is about human relations. Thus we can afford to be sorry for him in his foolishness.

To summarize, Shaw shows Higgins to be well-meaning and entirely free from malice. His misbehavior is so unconventional as to be funny. And also, he feels pain, as well as inflicts it, when his own emotions become involved. For all these reasons, we find Higgins likeable throughout the play.

Question: Explain how Alfred Doolittle contributes to the comic spirit of *Pygmalion*.

Answer: Alfred Doolittle, the philosophic dustman, has little connection with the main action of the play. But he does add a great deal of comedy to it.

He is a disreputable figure as he enters Higgins' house in Act II. He is dressed in the costume of his occupation, which is garbage-collecting. He has an hypocritical air of grave concern as he tells Higgins that he has come to rescue his daughter from Higgins' clutches. This pose collapses swiftly when Higgins tells him to take the girl home. Now he is revealed as a cheerful rogue. What he wants is a payment of five pounds for his daughter. He explains that he needs the money to get drunk on. He proceeds to explain his outlook on life, especially his own enjoyable but insecure position as one of the Undeserving Poor. His outlook is quite different from the usual moral attitude. He expresses it in dreadful slum English that is yet full of oratorical decorations. Higgins is so taken with him that he offers him ten pounds instead of five. It is an example of Doolittle's originality of outlook that he refuses. He might not have the heart to spend ten pounds. He leaves, contented with his loot.

The next time we see Doolittle, he is an unhappy bridegroom, elegantly attired in striped pants, tail coat, and top hat. An American millionaire has left him four thousand pounds a year. Doolittle bitterly discusses the consequences. He has become a helpless member of the middle class. He must pay large, unnecessary fees to doctors and lawyers. He must hire servants whether he wants them or not. He has become the financial support of a crowd of shiftless relatives. And his private life is no longer his own. He is about to marry Eliza's sixth stepmother. This poor woman's spirit is also broken. She is willing, for the first time, to get married. And she does not even have the heart to quarrel with anybody.

We may summarize by saying that whether he is on the scene as a cheerful scoundrel or as a miserable bridegroom, Doolittle enlivens the play with his unusual though anti-social ideas and his picturesque speech.

Question: Discuss the ending of the play. Whom will Eliza marry? Why?

Answer: If *Pygmalion* had a routine happy ending, Higgins would offer his heart to Eliza. Pygmalion would wed Galatea, and they would live happily ever after. This would be satisfying, but it would also be ordinary. The play would be agreeable but not very distinguished. Shaw shows that life is not as simple as such an ending would suggest. There are many complications in the relationship involving Eliza, Higgins, and Freddy.

Eliza admires Higgins. She cares for him. In fact, she tells him so. But his position in relation to her is that of the magician, or the sculptor who creates a lovely statue. He is almost godlike to her. This is not a comfortable basis for a day-to-day intimacy.

The final scene also suggests that Higgins cares for Eliza. He wants her to come back to Wimpole Street. To achieve this he is willing to coax her and be charming to her, just as he is to his mother or Mrs. Pearce when he wants something. But he will not do what must be done when a man wants a woman to share his life. He will not make himself vulnerable to her. He will not give up his self-sufficiency to express a deep need on her. He tries to eat his cake and have it. He wants her to come back without his making any emotional concessions. Thus he will have the comfort of her presence, but he will still belong entirely to himself. He, she, and Pickering will be three old bachelors together-a suggestion that is as pathetic as it is revelatory.

Shaw leaves the situation unsettled at the end of the play. We do not know whether Higgins will draw back and keep the existence he cherishes, or whether he will be impelled by his need to make the daring move toward another human being. Eliza waits for him to express his impulse toward her. He resists for the time being and she leaves. This is not necessarily final. The audience does not feel it as final. We still do not know whether Eliza will end up with this difficult but supremely interesting man who does not realize what has happened to his emotions. Perhaps she will accept instead the comforting adoration of Freddy. He is attractive and gentle, though not intelligent. And Higgins may not be able to break away from his settled ways and his devotion to his mother. Also, Eliza at her present stage of development is in some ways more than equal to Higgins. She knows him well enough to understand how to torment him. Note how he squirms as Eliza discusses his shortcomings placidly with his mother and Pickering. Perhaps Higgins will not want so frightening a companion. We do not know.

Shaw does not seem to have intended any further explanation about the ending. But the actor who portrayed Higgins in the original production made it clear from his behavior that Higgins was going to court Eliza in spite of Shaw's instructions. This so annoyed the author that he wrote an essay to be published with the play. In this, he states plainly that Eliza married Freddy, that they opened a flower shop, and that they were happy together. This is a believable ending for the play, but it is not the only possible ending.

PYGMALION

. . . .

PYGMALION

Ever since its original productions (it opened in seven different European capitals in various translations, after which it enjoyed a hugely successful production in London in 1914), *Pygmalion* has been one of Bernard Shaw's most popular plays. Not only have there been numerous stage productions of the play, but a film in 1938 and the overwhelmingly successful musical comedy adaptation of the 1950s *My Fair Lady* give evidence of its great vitality. Today more people are probably acquainted with *Pygmalion* in some form than with any other play by Shaw. Even Shaw's masterpiece, the towering Saint Joan, does not rival it in this respect.

Most critics agree that *Pygmalion* is a delightfully amusing, well-constructed comedy. Beyond this, their views diverge.

St. John Ervine, the Irish playwright, a friend and biographer of Shaw, judges that *Pygmalion* is not one of Shaw's major plays. He feels that its subject does not excite deep interest. Most audiences are not greatly impressed by the need for an improved alphabet. Yet Ervine gives credit to the play for its entertainment value. In other words, Ervine is one representative of those critics who find *Pygmalion* and amusing play but not an important one.

Ervine's opinion, of course, is based on his idea that the play is about the improvement of speech and the usefulness of a reformed alphabet in improving it. If the play is only about this, we may possibly agree that the play is trivial, that in it Shaw is concerned with a hobby that has a special interest for him but is of less concern to the majority of other people.

Yet we must note that some critics find a deeper **theme** in *Pygmalion*. Eric Bentley, in his study Bernard Shaw, finds in *Pygmalion* the story of the creation of an independent human being. In Acts II and III, Higgins makes a duchess of Eliza (although an imperfect one). In Acts IV and V, Eliza, moving from resentment to independence, makes a free woman of herself. Martin Meisel, author of the analytical study, Shaw and the Nineteenth Century Theater, regards the play as a radical attack on class distinction and class prejudice. He points out Eliza's final understanding that a flower girl and a duchess are distinguished from each other, not by their behavior., but by the way they are treated. Higgins carries this idea to a more far-reaching conclusion. He treats all women alike. He does not condescend to treat a flower girl a duchess; he treats duchesses like flower girls, thus destroying the whole notion of particular courtesy being due to certain people.

Archibald Henderson, who is considered to be the authoritative biographer of Shaw as well as an important critic of his work, also believes that *Pygmalion* is a statement of the idea that class barriers are artificial and must be broken down.

Another aspect of the play which has caused critical disagreement is its ending. Critics do not agree on what Shaw means the ending to be. They also do not agree on whether the present ending is suitable.

Many critics see the ending in the light of Shaw's concluding essay. They assume that Eliza must be walking out of Higgins' control and into Freddy's arms when she leaves Mrs. Higgins' drawing room. St. John Ervine is distressed by this possibility. He states his own conviction that Higgins marries Eliza, which is surely a tribute to the vitality and appeal of Shaw's characters. Ervine discusses them almost as if they were real people with a life of their own.

Eric Bentley accepts Eliza's marriage to Freddy. But to him her marriage is unimportant. The important thing is that she fights free of Higgins and becomes independent.

Martin Meisel is conscious of the difference between the ending of the play itself and the events described in Shaw's essay. Meisel points out that the play ends in a purposely ambiguous way. Shaw's flat statement that Freddy married Eliza came later and was provoked by the behavior of Sir Herbert Beerbohm Tree, who acted Higgins as a lovesick suitor in Act V. Meisel feels the ambiguity of the play is preferable to the definiteness of the essay. The point is that Eliza is now free to choose; whom she chooses is less important.

Arthur Nethercot gives still another interpretation of the ending in *Men and Supermen: The Shavian Portrait Gallery*. He feels Eliza's major concern is marriage. She wants to marry Higgins, but when she sees that Higgins is not a marrying man, she turns to Freddy, though he is a far less worthwhile person. This is a practical, sensible decision, but not idealistic. Nethercot refers to Eliza's choice of Freddy as "Philistine." She is pursuing woman who takes what she can as a husband.

To summarize, Shaw's play *Pygmalion* is considered by some critics to be a fairly unimportant comedy about speech improvement, while others see in it a significant attack on the absurdity of class distinction. All critics agree that it is an expert and amusing play. Most critics accept Shaw's essay on the ultimate marriage of Eliza and Freddy. But as Martin Meisel has pointed out, the play itself ends ambiguously. Some critics want to pair off Eliza and Higgins in marriage. Others feel that who Eliza marries does not matter to the **theme** of the play.

GENERAL REMARKS

There has been a great deal of criticism written about the life, work and thought of George Bernard Shaw. His career was long; he was exposed to criticism for over half a century during his own lifetime, and since his death in 1950, the commentary has continued. There is almost no drama critic who has not had his chance to write something about Bernard Shaw, for productions of Shaw's plays are unceasing. It is surprising that so little of this criticism is really intelligent or enlightening. It is well known that much criticism of Shaw is weak; Eric Bentley remarks upon this in his valuable short book, Bernard Shaw.

What are the reasons for this? Why is the criticism of Shaw less intelligent as a whole than the criticism of Shakespeare, for instance, when Shakespeare is a more puzzling and more intricate writer than Shaw?

One reason may well be Shaw's deceptive simplicity. He tries to write his plays very clearly, and often he even goes on to explain his purposes all over again in prefaces. Therefore, numerous critics of limited ability are very sure that they understand Shaw. But Shaw is not simple, even though he tries to be clear. In the first place, some of his theories are complicated. It is easy to understand them in a general way, but much harder to absorb all the details. Then too, it may be that Shaw could not explain himself completely, and like many great creative artists, he had certain qualities that he was unaware of himself. Thus, though he could explain what he meant to do, he could not always explain what he actually did do. A second factor is the anger Shaw arouses in many critics. They are troubled by his ideas and resentful of his self-confident and stinging expression of them. Anger and prejudice do not make a good basis for objective study. (Indeed, it is to be hoped that students will be the superiors of their elders in this. If Bernard Shaw expresses an opinion contrary to what a student believes, the student should remain calm, keep his mind open, and respect Shaw's opinion even if he cannot agree with it. This will often happen, for nobody accepts everything Shaw says, and some people accept very little of it. Above all, he should not fail to appreciate Shaw's writing because he happens to be unsympathetic to some of Shaw's thinking.)

SHAW'S IDEAS

Critical writing about Bernard Shaw usually discusses one or more of the following subjects: his ideas, his talent as a playwright, his writing style, and his life. The reader should try to be aware of any prejudices a critic may have as he reads. This is especially true of discussion about ideas. However, antagonism to Shaw's ideas sometimes affects other discussions, about his plays or his life, for instance.

Shaw's thinking is radical. His ideas on religion, sex, marriage, government, and money are therefore likely to startle or offend people who hold conservative views on any of these subjects. For example, St. John Ervine, an Irish playwright and a friend of Shaw, spends a great deal of space in his biography of Shaw *(Bernard Shaw: His Life, Work and Friends)* explaining why Shaw's socialism is wrong. He is especially concerned with the sameness and regimentation that socialism might create if it were to replace the capitalist economic system. He distrusts the mass of humanity. He is least friendly to those plays which have a large political or economic factor, such as *Major Barbara* and *The Apple Cart.*

Another man who was friendly with Shaw personally but critical of his ideas was Gilbert K. Chesterton. His book, *George Bernard Shaw* (1909), was one of the earliest studies of Shaw and his work, and as a result of Chesterton's own fine mind and witty expression, it is still one of the best. The book combines affectionate appreciation of Shaw's honesty, seriousness and independence with distress at the way Shaw rejects the usual ideas about sin and guilt, for Chesterton had a deeply religious nature himself and eventually became a Roman Catholic.

Shaw's discussions of sex have always created enemies. In the beginning of his career he was thought too outspoken; and early play, Mrs. Warren's Profession, completely broke the rules of censorship and could not be produced. Later the opposite was true. Certain writers who looked upon the sexual impulse as the basis of human behavior were shocked because Shaw felt that certain other parts of life (work, devotion to human betterment) were more important than sex. Among these writers were D. H. Lawrence and Frank Harris. They found him and his work lacking in sexuality and therefore incomplete. The American drama critic George Jean Nathan wrote an essay published in 1931 which lists all the places in his plays where the characters show a distrust or a dislike of sex. *Pygmalion* is mentioned. This essay is probably the least thoughtful expression of the idea of sex in Shaw's writing. It is reprinted by Louis Kronenberger in *George Bernard Shaw: A Critical Survey*.

There are also segments of Shaw's thought which are regarded by almost everyone as eccentric or wrongheaded. For example, his ideas on medicine seem cranky rather than critical. He does not have very much respect for the idea of germs. He is violently opposed to vaccination against smallpox. Then, too, some of his ideas are easy to make fun of, though on careful consideration, there is nothing silly about them. Shaw was a vegetarian. When he was in his forties, his health became poor for a while, and doctors told him it was absolutely necessary to begin eating meat. Shaw refused. He could not bring himself to eat the flesh of slaughtered fellow creatures. He wrote at the time that, if he did die, his funeral procession would consist of oxen, sheep, poultry, and even fish, all mourning the man who would rather die than eat them.

The gentle humor of the passage is touching. Looking back, one must respect the personal habits of a man who lived to be ninety-four years old. But it was easy for a critic who wanted to get an easy laugh in Shaw's lifetime to say that his plays would improve if he ate steak.

We may say, then, that comments on Bernard Shaw as a thinker range from the thoughtfully critical to the crudely hostile. But there are also writers who give a more balanced view of Shaw's ideas. A careful explanation may be found in Eric Bentley's *Bernard Shaw*.

SHAW THE PLAYWRIGHT

Discussion of Shaw as play-wright usually concerns his character portrayals. Most commentators agree on the liveliness and wit of the conversation in the plays, but they argue about whether the characters themselves are convincing human beings. Some critics claim that the characters do not have the complexity and warmth of real people. They are only types, or representations of ideas, rather than human beings. Archibald Henderson, the author of the most important biography of Shaw, believes this. He calls Shaw's characters "intellectual abstractions." Other critics feel that, while Shaw's characters are not absolutely realistic, Shaw is able to create a convincing manner of thought and speech for each of them. St. John Ervine says of Shaw's dialogue that it has "the rich tone of an unusual mind and yet is faithful to the nature of the people who speak it."

Homer E. Woodbridge, in *George Bernard Shaw, Creative Artist*, writes of the immense vividness of Shaw's portraits. He says that in Shaw's plays there is a group of unforgettable people who have become a living part of our literary heritage. Higgins, Eliza, and Alfred Doolittle are examples.

Some critics have also discussed the structure of Shaw's plays. Shaw himself pointed out in the preface to *Caesar and Cleopatra* that there is nothing new about the structure of his plays. He tells old stories in familiar ways. Only his ideas make his plays new.

Most critics agree with Shaw's own estimate. But to this they add the comment that even if Shaw's plays are not revolutionary, they are very competently put together. By this they mean that the plays tend to have a beginning, a middle, and an end, and that they move along at a quick pace with many interesting changes of mood and feeling. Only in his last plays did Shaw let his interest in ideas make his plays slow-moving and somewhat disorganized.

A useful study of Shaw with emphasis on dramatic structure is C.B. Purdom's *A Guide to the Plays of Bernard Shaw*. Purdom analyzes the fine points of structure in the plays.

SHAW'S STYLE

Critical comment and Shaw's writing style is overwhelmingly favorable. A few people do object to the sledge hammer forcefulness with which Shaw pounds home his ideas. Once critic says that there are no lyrical (poetic) passages in Shaw's plays. But almost every serious critic in his own way expresses admiration for Shaw's prose, which sounds simple, but which actually is a triumph of economy, clarity, and strength.

Eric Bentley remarks that to understand how much more than "simple Shaw's writing is, you need only see an ordinary Hollywood movie and a movie of a Shaw play in the same day. The flabbiness and flatness of the first give a clue to the control and force of the second. The modern poet W. H. Auden compares Shaw's writing to the music of Rossini, the great Italian composer of comic opera who wrote *The Barber of Seville*. Shaw has, he says, the same tunefulness, humor, vivacity and clarity in his words as the master composer has in his music.

SELECTED BIBLIOGRAPHY AND GUIDE TO FURTHER READING

Many plays by George Bernard Shaw are available in good paperback editions such as the Penguin editions. The Modern Library also has reprinted some of Shaw's plays. There is a three volume set of *Selected Plays* published by Dodd, Mead, and Company. Students should make sure that they secure a complete copy of a play; if there is a preface, it should be included. The following plays are of great interest:

For Shaw's discussion of the nature of love and the relationship between men and women—

Arms and the Man (1894)

Candida (1894)

Captain Brassbound's Conversion (1899)

Man and Superman (1901-1903)

For Shaw's theories about socialism—

Widowers' Houses (1892)

Mrs. Warren's Profession (1893)

Major Barbara (1905)

Shaw's historical plays—

The Devil's Disciple (1897)

Caesar and Cleopatra (1898)

Androcles and the Lion (1911)

Saint Joan (1923)

About Ireland—

John Bull's Other Island (1904)

About doctors and medicine—

The Doctor's Dilemma (1906)

Shaw's music criticism has been edited by Eric Bentley and published by Doubleday Anchor Books as a paperback under the title *Shaw on Music*. His drama criticism is reprinted as *Dramatic Opinions and Our Theatre in the Nineties* (complete). A later edition edited by A. C. Ward is called *Plays and Players*.

BOOKS ABOUT SHAW

BIOGRAPHY

Ervine, St. John. *Bernard Shaw: His Life, Work and Friends*. New York: William Morrow and Company, 1956.

The author, an Irish playwright and friend of Shaw, is sympathetic to Shaw as a person but criticizes his ideas at great length. The personal details about Shaw's life are much more interesting than the criticism.

Henderson, Archibald. *George Bernard Shaw: Man of the Century*. New York: Appleton-Century-Crofts, Inc. 1956.

The most complete biography of Shaw.

Pearson, Hesketh. *G.B.S., A Full Length Portrait*. New York and London: Harper and Brothers, 1942.

Contains an excellent selection from Shaw's correspondence.

CRITICAL STUDIES

Bentley, Eric. *Bernard Shaw, 1856-1950*. Norfolk, Connecticut: New Directions Books, 1947, revised 1957.

Valuable especially for Bentley's careful explanation of Shaw's ideas. First edition written when Shaw was still alive, and was called *Bernard Shaw*.

Kronenberger, Louis. ed. *George Bernard Shaw: A Critical Survey*. Cleveland and New York: The World Publishing Company, 1953.

A wide selection of essays on Shaw, covering many aspects of his life and work.

MacCarthy, Desmond. *Shaw*. London: Macgibbon and Kee, 1951.

The author, one of the foremost drama critics of his day, here puts together the reviews and discussions of Shaw's plays which he wrote during his long career.

Meisel, Martin. *Shaw and the Nineteenth Century Theater.* Princeton: The Princeton University Press, 1963.

A study tracing the relationship between Shaw's plays and the conventional stage plays of his time.

Nethercot, Arthur H. *Men and Supermen: The Shavian Portrait Gallery.* Cambridge: The Harvard University Press, 1954.

Analysis of Shaw's characters.

Purdom, C. B. *A Guide to the Plays of Bernard Shaw.* London: Methuen and Company, Limited, 1963.

A discussion of the structure, characters, and production of each play.

Woodbridge, Homer E. *George Bernard Shaw, Creative Artist.* Carbondale: Southern Illinois University Press, 1963.

A study which evaluates Shaw as a poor thinker but a great playwright.

SHAW ANTHOLOGIES

Wilson, Edwin, ed. *Shaw on Shakespeare.* New York; E. P. Dutton and Company, Inc. 1961.

A collection of Shaw's comments on Shakespeare, including the reviews of Shakespeare's plays he wrote while a drama critic.

Winsten, Stephen, ed. *The Quintessence of G.B.S.* New York: Creative Age Press, 1949.

A collection of various comments from Shaw's plays, prefaces, and essays arranged according to subject. Pleasant to browse in.